IN THE EYE OF A STORM

45 Days of Turbulence and Peace

Dr. Rico D. Short

The LEEP Group LLC

©2019 Dr. Rico D. Short. All rights reserved.

No part of this book may be reproduced, stored in a retrieval system, or transmitted by any means without the written permission of the author.

First published by Amazon 12/10/19

Printed in the United States of America

I would like to dedicate this book first of all to my wife Angela. She has been so supportive of me during this very difficult time of my life. To my children Ava and Jayla thanks for not giving up hope on your dad. I know this has been a very scary moment for you but God always has a plan. To my mother Shirva thanks for all the love and support through my whole life and never stopped beleiving in me. To the rest of my family, friends, staff, and colleagues thanks for all you have done for me and my family. I pray this book be of value to you and your family 100 years from now. I love all of you!

- Rico

PREFACE

What Happened?.....

◆ ◆ ◆

School had just started back in session from the very short summer break. The kids were very anxious and was ready for another break. Fall break was upon the horizon. I discussed with my family various options for vacation. They decided to go to Lake Lanier right outside of Atlanta, Georgia to spend our fall break. That's when everything changed. My life went into a turbulent tailspin. On September 28, 2019, I had a very serious eye injury at Lake Lanier riding down a water slide.

As I was sliding down, I felt my body hydroplane off the slide. Because I was afraid I was possibly going to fly off the slide or into water, I held my nose and braced myself for impact. As I crashed into the other part of the slide, my right thumb protruded deep into my left eye socket. It was the worst pain ever. I thought my eyeball had come out of its socket and I was blind. Fortunately it didn't come out but my left eye was severely injured. I was rushed by ambulance to the hospital. The doctors were able to stabilize me at the hospital but my left eye sustained possible career ending injuries. Over 20 years devoted to my passion of dentistry could be all gone down the drain.

As a dentist or endodontist to be more specific this injury caused my life to take a turn into some turbulent waters.

Would I ever practice again?
How am I going to take care of my family?
Will I lose my practice?
Will I lose everything I've worked so hard for?

These were just a few questions I have had to ask myself while on this eye injury journey. These 45 days are key moments in which I had to find "Peace In The Eye Of A Storm".

"Regardless of what happens in life, Jesus said "If you continue in my word you will know (perceive, understand, become intimate with) The Truth (who is me), and The Truth will make you free. So if the Son makes you free (vs your own self effort), you will be free indeed (won't ever go back to stay in that fallen mindset of religion or works again)."

"The devil's intention was to kill mankind's awareness of their god-identity. He was a thief from the beginning. He doesn't want your stuff. He'll even let you keep your religion. He's after the way you think about yourself in the light of God. He wants to try to convince you that God isn't good all the time by bringing up your past and using all the distractions around you now."

- DR. RICO D. SHORT

TABLE OF CONTENTS

Day #1 - Gratitude Rewires Your Brain

Day #2 - Our Weak Areas

Day #3 - The Lord Will See You Through

Day #4 - This Is Only A Test

Day #5 - Laugh Away The Disappointment

Day #6 - Many Are Called But Few Are Chosen

Day #7 - Worship While You Wait

Day #8 - It Will Turn Around

Day #9 - Overcoming Trouble Within And Without

Day #10 - It's Not Always Going To Be Like This

Day #11 - Praise Him In The Valleys Not Just The Mountain Top

Day #12 - Problems Are Only Temporary

Day #13 - Keep Your Hope In The Lord

Day #14 - Whose Report Are You Going To Believe?

Day #15 - Hope Is Never Lost

Day #16 - Trust Him When You Can't Trace Him

Day #17 - The God Of Grace

Day #18 - God Is Up To Something

Day #19 - God Is Present

Day #20 - He Has Started A Good Work

Day #21 - Temporary Tears

Day #22 - Full Speed Ahead

Day #23 - You Have The Creator Inside Of You

Day #24 - Joy & Pain

Day #25 - God Hears Us

Day #26 - The Winds of Change

Day #27 - When Your Brook Dries Up

Day #28 - Being Stable As The World Turns

Day #29 - What If...

Day #30 - Walking Through The Haze Of Change

Day #31 - Trusting Him 100%

Day #32 - Prince of Peace

Day #33 - Keep Doubt Out

Day #34 - Let The Lord Fight For You

Day #35 - A Miracle In Transition

Day #36 - Mind Games

Day #37 - Waves Of Doubt

Day #38 - The Panic Button

Day #39 - Count It ALL Joy?

Day #40 - Rejoice in the Lord—Always....In All Ways?

Day #41 - Entrust Your Trial To The Judge

Day #42 - Think On The Truth

Day #43 - The Waiting Period

Day #44 - Created Fearless

Day #45 - The Number 45

DAY #1

Gratitude Rewires Your Brain

❖ ❖ ❖

In life we encounter things that make us very happy and things that make us very upset. My eye injury has been one of those situations that was making me bitter. It's very dangerous to live with a mind full of remorse and bitterness. However, what do you do when facing a situation you can't change? Did you know we can erase the negativity and bitterness from our mind? Neuroscience has revealed gratitude can literally rewire our brain cells to be happier.

According to UCLA's Mindfulness Awareness Research Center, regularly expressing gratitude literally changes the molecular structure of the brain, keeps the gray matter functioning, and makes us healthier and happier. When you feel happy, the central nervous system is affected tremendously.

You are more peaceful, less reactive, and less resistant to interact with others. Studies show you desire to exercise more, lose weight, and even desire to eat healthier which translates to longer life.

Who wouldn't want that in their daily routine? In addition gratitude is associated with better sleep, less anxiety, less depression, and even relying on less medication. This can also save a lot of money in the future. This savings can create a nest egg for retirement. Gratitude or simply being thankful is the most effective practice for stimulating feelings of happiness.

Three simple steps to becoming more grateful

1. Start by praying.

How has your prayer life been lately? Praying is like your kidneys that filter all the toxins from your body. Prayer is like the blood running through your spiritual veins. Prayer is an unseen force. Prayer is the protective force around our lives. It positions us in a place of power. It positions us in a place of rest. **We should never ever underestimate the power of prayer in our own lives.** Prayer is an indicator of the health of our relationship with God. Whether praying in the natural or your spiritual tongue it gets all of heaven's attention. It creates communication to the unseen heavenly world like Wi-Fi connections. **Prayer guards our spirit.** Prayer is a secret place, an uncelebrated place, at times a painful place, but it is a crucial place.

Ask yourself this question: What does my prayer life look like right now? Am I putting myself in a place of power through prayer or am I, through my lack of connection to God, putting myself in a place of vulnerability to the attack and the weapons of the enemy?

2. Being thankful.

If you've only got time to say one prayer today, make it the simple words of *"thank you."* It does not matter if you are facing a giant mountain or a giant Goliath.

This is worth keeping in mind as you go about figuring out your daily practices and routines. It has helped me during this eye injury journey tremendously.

Keep a daily journal of three things you are thankful for daily. This works well first thing in the morning, or just before you go to bed.

3. **Complimenting yourself and others.**

Make it a practice to tell a spouse or friend something you appreciate about them every day. This creates a sense of self-worth and rewires your brain. Look in the mirror when you are brushing your teeth and think about something you have done well recently or something you like about yourself.

NOTES

DAY #2

Our Weak Areas

God's Grace can only work in areas you are weak in. His Grace isn't in your strengths. Therefore we can glory in our weakness because he's there for us in them! Paul explained this in 2 Corinthians 12 very eloquently. Paul received many extravagant revelations of God, Jesus, Angels, and more during his ministry. The crazy thing He wasn't one of the OG's or original 12 disciples. In fact, he use to persecute Christians as a legalistic Pharasitic Jew. He also knew The Law backwards and forwards. With this kind of knowledge it would be very easy to get "the big head" or arrogant and insensitive.

Listen what Paul says ...

> *"Because of the extravagance of those revelations, and so I wouldn't get a big head, I was given the gift of a handicap to keep me in constant touch with my limitations."*

He called his handicap a gift. Man you talk about speaking faith! How many of us look at our handicap or shortcomings as a gift? Guess what it does? It keeps on our spiritual knees and keeps our dependence on God!

Check out what else Paul said..

> "Satan's angel did his best to get me down; what he in fact did was push me to my knees. No danger then of walking around high and mighty!"

There are many dark forces trying to keep us from receiving God's best. They may be internal or they may be external. It may be a fallen mindset. It may be some religious system that has oppressed you. It may be something on the outside. A person. A physical challenge, etc. Sometimes they seem overwhelming. **But nothing can stand in the way of the grace of God for us.** You may be down right now. Your vision may be blurry physically like mine, mentally, or emotionally. But in a little while you will be able to see clearly and get back up on your feet again!

It was interesting to hear Paul say that he didn't think of it as a gift at first. Like we all do in the natural!

> "At first I didn't think of it as a gift, and begged God to remove it. Three times I did that, and then he told me, My grace is enough; it's all you need. My strength comes into its own in your weakness".

It was in the spirit by faith Paul called his handicap a gift! **Sometimes we beg God to remove the thing that's going to make us stronger and more dependent on him.** We ask him over and over again like Paul did three times. But the beauty of it is Grace will conquer all our weaknesses and shortcomings in Christ Jesus. That's something we can throw a party about! That's something we can celebrate extravagantly!

Check out what Paul said next...

> "Once I heard that, I was glad to let it happen. I quit focusing on the handicap and began appreciating the gift."

He just threw in the towel as an act of total surrender! This is when you are all in! **See you have to take your eyes off your limitations and place them on the one who will never fail!** *Grace flows when you let go.* I'm going to repeat that. **<u>Grace flows when you let go!</u>** That's when Christ moves in and "take the wheel".

This kind of behavior actually changes your attitude about the situation you are facing. It takes all the focus off of you and put them on Jesus! Paul finally says...

> "Now I take limitations in stride, and with good cheer, these limitations that cut me down to size—abuse, accidents, opposition, bad breaks. I just let Christ take over!"

Are you willing to let Christ take over? Do you think he needs your help? Well he doesn't! Many times he want you to sit down, relax, and receive! See when Christ takes over everything changes.

So maybe you have been abused, maybe you've been an accident and have a handicap temporarily or permanently, facing a very challenging situation in your marriage your finances or your health. It seems like you can't catch a good break. If you keep your trust in Jesus he will turn your mountain into a miracle! And so remember in your weakness that's where your greatest miracle and ministry will be birth. Finally Paul said...

> "And so the weaker I get, the stronger I become."

DR RICO D SHORT

You are strong in the Lord fam. There will be glory after this! (2 Corinthians 12:7-10 MSG)

NOTES

DAY #3

The Lord Will See You Through

Jesus performed three ocular miracles. According to the New Testament, Jesus cured blind men in Jericho, Bethsaida and Siloam.

The blind man at Jericho
With reference to the blind man named Bartimaeus at Jericho. Jesus told him to receive your sight because of his faith in Luke 18:35.

The blind man at Bethsaida
Matthew mentions two blind men healed because of their faith in Matthew 9:29. Jesus touched their eyes and healed them. However in Mark 8:22 Jesus put spit on a man's eyes at Bethsaida and healed him.

The blind man at Siloam
In John Chapter 9 Jesus healed a blind man who was blind from birth. Jesus **spit on the ground, made some mud with the saliva,**

and put it on the man's eyes. He told him, "wash in the Pool of Siloam". So the man went, washed, and came home seeing.

Hebrews 13:6 says

> *"God assures us, I'll never let you down, never walk off and leave you, I'm ready to help; therefore you can be fearless no matter what!"*

We know no matter who or what has plotted against us; God promises to SEE us through! Especially what I'm going through with my eye injury, I need to see everything through Jesus lens of **Grace & Faith.**

Whether on our jobs, within our relationships, in our health, in our finances, or while in school, we can trust God is there to help us. It must be more than a feeling. It's gotta be a matter of fact. Just like you're reading this and breathing. God is so good to us! He's a very present help in time of trouble (Psalm 46:1). We do not have to be fearful because God has already promised victory in our battles! The Lord will SEE us through!

> *"If your faith remains strong, even while surrounded by life's difficulties, you will continue to experience the untold blessings of God! True happiness comes as you pass the test with faith and receive the victorious crown of life promised to every lover of God!"*

James (Jacob) 1:12 TPT

Reflection: Think about a time you worried about an issue and God gave you victory. Remember, He is the same God yesterday, today and tomorrow. He will certainly help you once again!

DR RICO D SHORT

NOTES

DAY #4

This Is Only A Test

◆ ◆ ◆

"This is only a test!" So often, we hear these words during the late-night hours via our televisions or during the day while an amber alert is being rehearsed. Please understand these great words can also be applied to our lives as well. Read Philippians 4:11-12. These scriptures remind us to remain content.

Each and every day as we go through the journey of life, God is testing us to see if we are ready for a promotion. As a result, we are often confronted by trials and tribulations where God is testing us to see how we will respond. Remember, this is only a test! Refer to Proverbs 3:25-26, it reminds us not to be afraid but to be confident in the Lord. Here are four other powerful scriptures that will help you in your time of testing.

1. "Anyone who meets a testing challenge head-on and manages to stick it out is mighty fortunate. For such persons loyally in love with God, the reward is life and more life."

(James 1:12 MSG)

2. "Blessed is the man who keeps on going when times are hard. After he has come through them, he will receive a crown. The crown is life itself. God has promised it to those who love him."
(James 1:12 NIRV)

3. "Peace I leave with you; My [perfect] peace I give to you; not as the world gives do I give to you. Do not let your heart be troubled, nor let it be afraid. [Let My perfect peace calm you in every circumstance and give you courage and strength for every challenge.]"
(JOHN 14:27 AMP)

4. "Stop allowing yourselves to be agitated and disturbed; and do not permit yourselves to be fearful and intimidated and cowardly and unsettled."
(John 14:27 AMPC)

Your mind is so powerful and amazing! It dictates to your heart, your body, and your daily life. Do you know you can literally think yourself into supernatural confidence or paralyzing fear, a state of continuous momentum or grounded immobility, a state of blissful happiness or a sense of hopelessness?

Jesus desires for us to be anxious for nothing, to live in perfect peace and confidence. You only can do that by keeping your eyes on Him and off the situation at hand. Remember Peter? When his eyes were fixed on Jesus he literally walked on water. When they got fixed on the trouble around him aka the winds and waves of life, he started sinking.

We have been warned that troubles in this life will come, that there will be trials of many kinds, but we have something special as Believers! We must choose to fix our eyes on the author and finisher of our faith - Jesus! When we do that we get his perfect peace not the world's shallow idea of peace. We must deliberately choose how we think and how we see Jesus in our situation. Then either our situation will change or we will change in the midst of our situation.

Prayer
Daddy God...Enlarge my capacity to receive this measure of Your life and your mindset during this test I'm facing. Lord, not as the world knows the high life, but the higher life in Christ. Amen.

NOTES

DAY #5

Laugh Away The Disappointment

◆ ◆ ◆

Life presents many reasons for us to worry, to doubt and to deeply reflect, and questions seem to outweigh the answers. *Why did I get this sickness, Why am I struggling financially, Why am I depressed, Why did I lose a loved one, Why did I get a divorce, Why did I lose my job, Why did I have this eye injury that's jeopardizing my career in dentistry and providing for my family?* It makes us all wonder how can God be "good all the time"?

See Beloved, what we see with our natural eyes does not always line up with our interpretation of the Bible. Remember the story of Job? His loss? And yet through it all, we must believe, maintain and strengthen our faith, trusting implicitly that **God makes everything beautiful in its time**. Remember Job! His triumphant ending!

The fact of the matter is God lives outside of time. **He is Eternal and All Knowing.** God is all-in-all and He knows exactly what He is doing in and through your life. It's only been 2 weeks since my eye injury but it feels like 2 years! Did you know with Job his trial only lasted a few months max? Then God restored his health, possessions, children more than double in quality and quantity!

Life can at times seem harsh and unfair, and circumstances can frustrate us. But the truth remains: **God makes it all beautiful in His perfect time.** Read that again! There is a divine thread that runs through our times and seasons. The thread is Jesus Grace and Mercy. So Just go with it!

If you ever thought that life in Christ was meant to be dreary, severe and somber, read Ecclesiastes 3:12–13 (CSB):

> *"I know that there is nothing better for them than to rejoice and enjoy the good life. It is also the gift of God whenever anyone eats, drinks, and enjoys all his efforts."*

There is indeed nothing better for us than to be *joyful*. If you lack joy, ask Jesus for some of His. Joy is stable not subject to what's happening to us. See Happiness depends on the environment. **Joy is a God-emotion and laughter that should be a natural part of our daily life**. So when trouble comes your way, like my eye injury or worse choose joy! Trade your worry for happiness and watch God Work all things together for your good!

> *Did you know God loves laughter? Psalm 24 says "Heaven-throned God breaks out laughing, Today, choose to laugh away the blues!*

NOTES

DAY #6

Many Are Called But Few Are Chosen

◆ ◆ ◆

The Bible tells us that many are called but few are chosen. I believe this verse is referring to our calls in the Lord, not to our personal salvation in Him. Salvation is free for everyone who Believes in Jesus! The term chosen I believe is different. For instance there are many dentists that can do root canals well. Then they are dental specialist "called" Endodontist that have the training to do root canals at a high level exclusively. But there are the "chosen" ones like a Board-Certified Endodontist to do them at the highest level, publish articles, volunteer, give back, mentor, lecture, have a passion for excellence, teaching others in a thought-provoking way, and representing the kingdom of God at the same time. These are the chosen ones! Or maybe I'm just a little biased because they describe me...lol.

However, the chosen ones don't have glitz and glamor all the time. Life happens to all of us. Even the chosen ones. Look at me and my eye injury. I am visually impaired. I can't practice. I have no income currently. My family is depending on me. It's a dark and lonely time for me in the natural. However the opposite is true in the spiritual realm.

The chosen at times will feel totally alone, depending on the type of calling that God has placed on their life and exactly where they are in the development of that calling.

The good news is the great men of faith felt the same way at times.
For example:

- David was alone when he took on Goliath. No one else would step on the battlefield with him when he took on that evil blasphemous giant.

- Peter was alone when he stepped out of the boat to walk on water, as the Bible says that the rest of the apostles were too scared to try and do it on their own.

- Moses was all by himself for 40 years in the backside of the desert before God called him out to deliver the Israelites from Egypt.

- David was hiding out in caves from Saul for quite a number of years before he was finally called out to become the greatest king of Israel.

At times, you may feel totally isolated and alone at the spot where God may have you at. For me it was a freak accident at a water park just trying to have fun with my kids. I ask the question...

"God where were you?"

You know how I need my eyes for my occupation and to provide for my family. How could you let this happen to one of your chosen! Then He says settle down son. I have a plan! It's going to be amazing what I'm going to show this world through you and this dry time!

Did you know we are designed spiritually like an eagle? The Bible says those that wait on the Lord shall renew their strength and mount up in wings like an eagle. The wings symbolize strong relationships and the undying love of God. Because the eagle is a symbol of strength, and because their hunt brings them prosperity, they are also the preferred guardians for businesses. In addition, eagles have wings that are long and broad, to help them soar and glide with less effort....aka the ***Grace Life!*** At low speeds, broad wings can hold the eagle in the air longer like standing in midair....***The Anointing***! And broad wings provide extra lift when an eagle has to carry its prey up into the air with less effort...***The Favor!***

When you are in these kinds of dry times and seasons with the Lord, just keep pressing forward and flying alone like the eagle does – and sooner or later God will bring you forth into the heart of your call where everyone will then see you and work with you on the call that God has placed on your life. For me it may still be my passion of Endodontics or something bigger!

NOTES

DAY #7

Worship While You Wait

◆ ◆ ◆

Today is another day. Another day out of my practice. Another trip back to the doctor. Unfortunately things with my eye has not changed much. So I'm still waiting on my breakthrough.

One of the most beautiful keys I've learned as a Believer is to **worship while you wait for the breakthrough**. Worship, whether it be in the form of singing, whispering, meditating or resting in God's presence, is the most beautiful use of time while you wait. It's a safe place. It takes your focus off the situation or the delay and places it on the One who makes all things beautiful in His time (see Ecclesiastes 3:11).

You may not have an eye injury like me and your business is at a standstill. No one has any clear-cut answers. What are you in need of...Direction? Healing? Finance? Relationships? Business Advice?
The secret to receiving whatever you need is unlocked when we worship the Eternal One. Something magnificent happens when He becomes the most important of all people and things in your

life. ***You let go and let God have his way.*** Worship eventually becomes a strong desire and you will want to pursue Him like a deer that pants by the stream. Worship helps you learn to speak the language of His heart and while you wait, God is at work on your behalf, working all things together for your good (see Romans 8:28), and always at the right time!

Be still, and know that He is God, we are told in Psalm 46:10.

If you believe this, then you can be entirely dependent on Him. You can find the place of quiet in the depths of your heart. **It's a secret place that God places in every human being.** When the world's calamities are swirling around you and the storms surround you on every side, you can still have peace of mind. Rather than worry, be encouraged to worship—to keep your eyes and your heart focused and dependent on Jesus. *That's exactly what I'm doing during this eye injury.*

NOTES

DAY #8

It Will Turn Around

◆ ◆ ◆

Have you been dealing with a situation for a long period of time? I have! I am still in the middle of the storm. It's the 4th week since my eye injury. Still can't practice. Still have impaired vision. However, I am confident things will turn around! You may say doc how do you know for sure? There is a scripture that says,

> "For I know that this shall turn to my salvation through your prayer, and the supply of the Spirit of Jesus Christ" (Philippians 1:19 KJV).

In other words I know that the lavish supply of the Spirit of Jesus and your prayers for me will bring about my deliverance. No matter what, I will continue to put my faith in Jesus finished work and follow the Holy Spirit as my counselor and guide. In the end God will get the glory and He will be openly revealed through me before everyone's eyes. So I will not be ashamed of the gospel of Jesus Christ!

Beloved, it does not matter how it looks today in your health, relationships, business, or finances, or even how it feels. God promises in His Word through prayer and praising, things will certainly turn around.

We know this is true because in Isaiah 55:11 it states,

> *"So shall My word be that goes forth out of My mouth: it shall not return to Me void [without producing any effect, useless], but it shall accomplish that which I please and purpose, and it shall prosper in the thing for which I sent it."*

So you must be speaking the same words that God speaks over you! So say these 3 things continually: **"I am well. I am prosperous. I am delivered."**

If there is ever a time to really pray and believe, it is when you have been counted out, a relationship looks dead, a health situation when doctors have no answers, an opportunity seems too far to obtain or something seems hopeless! Make a commitment to keep praying, believing, and speaking life into that situation! God did not bring you this far to dump you on the curb. No! You are more than a conqueror through Christ who loves you!

I challenge you to continue to pray about the situation, praise through the situation, speak life into the situation and no matter how hard it looks, God will turn it around in His time.

NOTES

DAY #9

*Overcoming Trouble
Within And Without*

Today I will be going to the office to speak to my staff about my eye situation. Unfortunately, there hasn't been any change in my vision. However, I must assure them that everything will work out fine! I know it's really difficult for many to understand how things like this can happen to people of faith.

Jesus taught that we would have trouble in this world. Each day would have enough trouble of its own. Not only will the world bring us trouble, but we have trouble residing within. Even when we have believed on the Lord Jesus Christ and accepted Him as our Lord and Savior trouble will come. So we don't have to go anywhere to find trouble. ***Trouble is within and without.*** Is there any hope?! YES! If you are in Christ, you are a new creation. You are in this world but you have a different "operating system". He is in you and you are in Him. ***Because He lives inside of you, there can be calm within despite what's going on outside.***

The truth of God and His Word is our anchor in the storm. Jesus spoke to the storm and it obeyed. Have you spoke to your storm lately? That's a true treasure that is inside of us as well! In Psalm 103 David instructs his soul to praise the LORD and bless His name. He reminds himself who he is and reminds himself not to forget who God is. We must do the same especially when facing trouble in our health, finances, career, marriage, and relationships! We must keep our minds fixed on the truth of God's Word and understand we are more than conquerors in Christ.

So today see yourself in the hands of God wrapped in the arms of Jesus. Meditate on that. Close your eyes. Can you see it? Can you feel the peace? It's a sweet spirit to know everything is gonna be fine. When we do this we will begin to experience the calm of Christ that he promises.

NOTES

DAY #10

It's Not Always Going To Be Like This

◆ ◆ ◆

Yesterday I went in for an MRI on my eye. We will make a decision next week on a surgical procedure. My vision hasn't changed externally but internally it has. How? Because I know God is working behind the scenes to make all things new! I don't care how the odds are stacked against me; I'm going to believe my best is yet to come! I know it will not always be this way. Romans 4:16-17 tells us through our faith and His grace the promise will be fulfilled in our lives. The promise is God's best and His perfect will for our lives. It also tells us it will be because of His grace we will receive the promise not our religious works!

See I grew up in a single parent home. My mother was a mill worker in the textile industry. She worked very hard long shifts. Her supervisor would often call her at 3am for a 5am shift after she's already worked 8 hours. She came home with cotton all over her. I witnessed my mother making many sacrifices to make ends meet. I remember her buying a box of Churches Chicken and that would be her lunch for the entire week. Our dinner sometimes were red link sausage sandwiches. Often times, we had to defend off roaches in our home. Despite all of this, she constantly believed we would succeed no matter what. For this reason, she never gave up!

After a while, her prayers were answered. I graduated from college, dental school, specialist school and became a very successful endodontist, author, professor, and speaker. Consistently, God has continued to bless her and now she just got married for the first time at age 64! These days, she does not have to worry about making ends meet. In fact, she often blesses me!

So, whatever you are expecting to turn around put the words into the atmosphere. ***Declare dead situations to turn around and live again!*** See it in your spirit. Death and life are in the power of the tongue. Begin to recite scriptures that relate to your situation daily.

Think about your journey in life and what God has saved you from. This isn't the first time I had to walk through a dark valley. I have experience with the Master so I know what I'm talking about! Meditate on how God has rescued you from tough times. Know because He is such an awesome God, and loves you unconditionally, He will do it again! I will see again. I will practice again. I will declare the works of the Lord again!

NOTES

DAY #11

*Praise Him In The Valleys Not
Just The Mountain Top*

◆ ◆ ◆

It's easy to praise God on the mountain top. But what about in the valley? Just recently, God instructed me to listen to praise and worship music during this eye injury journey. There has been times of fear, anxiety, and uncertainty but one thing remains steady is his love and faithfulness. This music has calmed me down and increased my faith. God said, begin to praise as if it has already happened…your eyes being perfectly restored, your practice taken care of, and you go to a higher level in me and your community! So that's what I've been doing lately…dancing like David did but my clothes haven't fallen off! Lol…**See we must learn how to Praise Him in the valleys and not just on the mountain top.**

I remember the scriptures speak of Paul and Silas who were put into jail for proclaiming the great works of God. If you've been following me for some time you know that's what I've been doing for years. Open your spiritual eyes to see this. Being placed in jail represents the trials and tribulations we too face today. Kind of where I am currently with my eye injury situation. At times I feel hopeless because I can't work and provide for my family. Like a prisoner who can't be of much help in a cell.

However, I'm encouraged that Paul and Silas did not view their situation as hopeless, but they praised God instead for what he has done and what he was going to do. They praised God with such an awesome power that all the prisoners throughout the jail heard their praise. ***And suddenly*** there was a great earthquake (a **shift in position** from the spiritual to the natural) the prison began to shake and all the doors opened and each prisoner's band loosen including theirs. Their trial was over and they were free! Their bands represented their health being tied up, their finances being tied up, their marriage being tied up, their business being tied up, etc.

Beloved whatever you are going through whether it's in your health, in your finances, on your job, in your marriage, or in your business start now to praise God in advance! This confuses the enemy....***and suddenly***, you will see your mountains being leveled and your crooked places made straight (Isaiah 45:2). I can't wait until this is over and give y'all my testimony! It's going to be awesome! Remember he's the God of the hills and valleys and you're never ever alone.

NOTES

DAY #12

Problems Are Only Temporary

◆ ◆ ◆

Problems in life are inevitable. They could be large or small. Whether it is a bad relationship, a failing marriage, a loved one that has been called home, financial distress, a bad doctor report, or a combination there are certain to be moments in life when you ask God, "Why?"
I've had many days like this since my eye injury. Like God you know me. We have a long history together! You know how much I love you. Why am I going through this?!

I have a question. Could God be using us to help someone else? If the battle was too big he would have never allowed it to happen to us. There are many disappointments in my life that I have overcome and they have always brought me out higher than before. Because of these experiences, I am now in a position to help others who may be experiencing similar issues and I am able to see them to victory, with God's help! 2 Corinthians 12:9 reminds us, His grace alone is sufficient! That's why I always hashtag #GraceLife in my posts. So, no matter what you are going through, God promises to see you through - full of Grace!

I know you may be saying Dr. Short this problem has been going on so long it seems permanent. ***<u>Beloved your feelings lie.</u>*** The Word says affliction is just for a moment (2 Corinthians 4:17). Another scripture reads - joy cometh in the morning (Psalm 30:5)! No matter what you are going through, you have to remain steadfast, trusting and believing God's Word is the same yesterday, today and tomorrow (Hebrews 13:8). In His Word, He promises He will never leave us or forsake us (Hebrews 13:5).

See Beloved, God has a divine strategy in this difficulty. Trust His strategy not your own!

We all have our own plans and desires. But God's plans for us are ***<u>always better and bigger!</u>*** Sometimes we do not understand the what, the how, and the why. We just need to understand The Who! God is The Who to see us through! The Word says Do not lean on your own understanding, but to His (Proverbs 3:5). Fam, Life isn't a sprint. It's a marathon with stops along the way. Life is like a long road, and your eyes can only see so far ahead. It can't see the turns, potholes, or forks in the road. However, God can see all the way down the road. In fact he's already at the end waiting for you to finish your race with an amazing prize! You automatically get 1st place because of Jesus finished work on your behalf!

So, when life takes you for an unexpected turn like an eye injury in my case and can't practice or things do not quite work out the way you envisioned, stand still and know God still cares for you. He's got this! Lift up your hands and continue to praise him for the victory coming! One day you will be able to say, God, I thank you for working all things together for good and seeing me through this! I have the victory!

NOTES

DAY #13

Keep Your Hope In The Lord

◆ ◆ ◆

When life gets hard it's easy to just lose hope and throw in the towel or raise the white flag and say I quit! Oh, I've felt like that many times during this eye injury journey. Thinking things like God, even when I performed root canals and surgery with 2 eyes it was very difficult at times. How in the world I'll be able to do it with one eye?

It may not be your eye. Your issue may be in your finances...like how you are going to pay your bills and you just got laid off. Or how are you going to live when your spouse just walked out on you. So often, we want to move at our own pace and try to fix the situation out of desperation or fear. Well let me just go in there and do a root canal or surgery with one eye! I got bills to pay and kids to feed God! Well let me go out there and work 3 jobs so I can maintain my household. Well let me go out and find a replacement spouse quickly because I don't like being alone.

These are all wrong responses to the problem.

Don't get ahead of what God is doing in this season. Instead move at his rhythm. Move at his pace. The unforced rhythm of

Grace.

> *Psalms 84 says "For the Lord God is a Sun and Shield; the Lord bestows PRESENT GRACE and FAVOR and FUTURE GLORY, HONOR, SPLENDOR, AND HEAVENLY BLISS TO ALL WHO WAITS PATIENTLY ON HIM!"*

God makes it clear that whatever you desire of Him, if you keep your hope in Him, He will renew your strength. In Joshua 1:5 I love the amplified translation. God says: [I will] not, [I will] not, [I will] not (3 times) in ANY degree leave you helpless nor forsake nor let you down nor relax My grip on you...Assuredly not! What a powerful promise we have!

I understand sometimes waiting on God can be challenging. Trust me I'm in the quiet storm right now. I don't know what God is doing in the background but I know he's working all things together for my good and your good! You may be saying like me, "God when? God why? God, what are you doing with me? God, I don't quite understand it. I don't like it!"

> *In these times we must remember God's word says, "No good thing will be withheld from you" (Psalms 84:11)*

While we are in the storm it is not for us to know the details of when, why or even to understand how long it will last. This is the only way to mature our faith. Faith is the currency of heaven. Get that! It's what "moves and motivates the hand of God". Not your tears or begging. If we are to see the spectacular and supernatural in this earth it will come in the form of employing our faith. Faith is the substance of things hoped for and the evidence of things not seen. If you know it and can see it then it's no longer faith in action. It's natural not supernatural. Through these trials and challenges, it is more relevant to understand He loves us so much He will not leave or forsake us (Hebrews 13:5). He will not withhold anything good from us (Psalm 84:11). Isn't this great to know!

> *I just want to remind you and myself that there is hope in your storm!*

If you find yourself waiting on God today, like me, let me encourage you to stand on God's Word. He knows you by name. He says there is hope in your future (Jeremiah 31:17). Just hold on a little while longer because your future is so bright! You will live a full life here on earth! Wait for Him and place all your hope in the Lord. In doing so, He will provide you with the strength to keep going and give you victory (Lamentations 3:26).

NOTES

DAY #14

*Whose report are you
going to believe?*

◆ ◆ ◆

It's day #14 and my vision still hasn't returned properly. I'm going in to see the surgeon today to figure out the next step. Should we wait and give it more time or jump in and do surgery in effort to try to correct the problem? In the meantime there has still been no income and bills are continuing to come. Thank God for savings but I know if there is no income, the savings will eventually run out. This is a valley experience for me and my family.

I have a choice to make. And that is Whose report am I going to believe?

In life, you will have at least one valley experience even as a Believer in Jesus. Jesus even had his share. I'm reminded that he was in the wilderness for 40 days and 40 nights with no food while the devil tested him. So likewise, as Believers we will have to walk through the valley of the shadow of death. Understand that it's only a shadow and it's just temporary.

The devil speak to you, saying things like you will not make it through this, your finances will dry up, your business won't make it, you will never overcome this addiction, your marriage won't last, your too old to get married, you're too fat, too skinny, too poor, not smart or even not beautiful enough. You must recognize these voices are of the devil not of God. God has made you beautiful, marvelous, and breathtaking. Psalm 139:14 says

> *"I thank you, God, for making me so mysteriously complex! Everything you do is marvelously breathtaking. It simply amazes me to think about it! How thoroughly you know me, Lord!"*

See God had the solutions before you had the problem.

See, I understand what you are going through. I'm still in my valley moment right now but I'm know I'm not alone. Jesus is there with me and he's with you. God already has a huge plan for my life and yours! I mean a big plan beyond our wildest dreams. The devil knows that too that's why he keeps messing with you. Don't believe the lies he's trying to construct in your head. He's the father of lies and there is no truth in him. God knows our future and more importantly He decrees we would have success!

Jeremiah 29:11 states,

> *"For I know the thoughts that I think toward you, saith the Lord, thoughts of peace, and not of evil, to give you a wonderful expected end."*

So how do you overcome these fiery darts that the enemy throws your way? You Fight back with God's Word!

> *"For the word of God is quick, and powerful, and sharper than any two-edged sword, piercing even to the dividing asunder of soul and spirit, and of the joints and marrow, and is a discerner of the thoughts and intents of the heart"* (Hebrews 4:12).

God's Word is the most powerful weapon you will ever own. <u>*It's more powerful than a nuclear bomb*</u>. Therefore, it is important to become acquainted with it. Memorize it. Study it. Treat it like food. You may find yourself in situations where your Bible may not be accessible and in order to obtain success, you must quickly fight back with the Word.

Not only you must know the Word, You must Speak The Word. Put it in the atmosphere!

Jesus had to do the same thing when he was tempted in the wilderness. You were made in the image and likeness of God. He spoke the world into existence so guess what you are going to have to do? Speak your finances into existence. Speak your healing into existence. Speak your business into existence. Speak your breakthrough into existence.

Make a commitment you will no longer allow the lies of the devil to linger. You must use spiritual weapons to fight spiritual things. We know the weapons of our warfare isn't carnal or in the natural. So declare God's Word over your situation. You will win each and every time.

The Holy Spirit said to me the devil didn't send you into this valley. I did. The same way I sent Jesus into the valley or wilderness. Just to let the devil know he was messing with God's child.

So are you. You're not going to die in the valley. I'm with you. Notice nobody ever died in the presence of Jesus!

See The valley is the gym of the Holy Spirit. It's where your spiritual muscles are made. See you are going to need them when I take on the mountain top. There's no gym there.

Goodness and Mercy is following you but if you keep running, worrying, trying to figure it out on your own...I can't catch up to you! Just sit down. Relax. Allow me to serve you says Jesus. That's why I came!

NOTES

DAY #15

Hope Is Never Lost!

◆ ◆ ◆

So often, when we face trials in life we want to lose hope. It's human nature. See it's easier to quit rather than stand on the promises of God. It seems like God isn't hearing our prayers or seems to slow to answer them. We get impatient, to be honest how I feel right now, and want to move at our own pace. Maybe I can inject someone with double vision, do a root canal with one eye, perform a surgery as well. Nahhh. I wouldn't want anyone to operate on me like that! In times like these want to move at our own pace but don't want to move at God's.

God makes it clear that whatever you desire of Him, if you keep your hope in Him, be patient, let Him work, He will renew your strength and you will come out of the fire higher without the smell of smoke!

I get it through. Sometimes waiting on God can be challenging. Heck all the time. **Did you know Jesus was never in a hurry to do anything. He walked everywhere and took his sweet ole time.** Ironically, Jesus said if you've seen me you've seen the Father who sent me. Well woomp there it is. He may not come when you want him but he'll be there...........just finish it for me!

You may be asking like me right now, "God what are you doing? God why are you allowing this? God how long is this going to last? God, I don't quite understand it." It is not for us to know when, why or even to understand His plans for our lives. It is more relevant to understand He loves us so much He will not leave or forsake us (Hebrews 13:5). He even loves us so much that He processes our pain for future pleasure!

Through all these questions you must remember Psalms 84:11 says

> *"For the LORD God is a sun and shield; The LORD bestows grace and favor and honor; No good thing will He withhold from those who walk uprightly."*

That's an amazing promise! You may be saying well I haven't been walking uprightly lately. I still got issues, sins, addictions, etc. Well good! Then You are a candidate for **Grace** and because of your faith in Jesus finished work God looks at you as spotless, blameless, and walking uprightly!! He will not withhold anything good from us! Isn't this great to know? God Is Always Good!

So if you find yourself today waiting on that financial breakthrough, waiting to get married, or for the marriage to turn around, that good report from your doctor, that raise or promotion on your job, waiting for your eye to be healed like me you can be assured that it's on the way if you continue to stand on His Word. God says there is hope in your future and He'll make beauty out of your ashes! (Jeremiah 31:17).

Just hold on a little while longer, put a smile on your face, put a pep in your step, and laugh uncontrollably knowing you will live a full vibrant life here on earth. Jesus said I've came to bring you life and life more abundantly to the full until it overflows! Wait for Him and place all your hope in the Lord. In doing so, He will provide you with the strength to keep going and give you victory. We are more than conquerors through Christ who gives us strength!

NOTES

DAY #16

Trust Him When You Can't Trace Him

◆ ◆ ◆

When you trace something you can see patterns and lines to follow. Unfortunately life isn't like that most of the time. Sometimes, we face life's issues in the dark and feel alone. We question where is God? We wonder why God has not stepped in. It feels that way but His Word says that He will never leave us or forsake us. In fact, He's inside of us working all things together for good. We may not see it or even feel it but it's happening. See you can't see or feel a Bluetooth signal or Wi-Fi signal but they are powerful because they can make many things work seamlessly.

It's day #16 since my eye accident and this keeps me encourage. I have a question, what if God has already helped us, would you believe it without seeing it? Beloved, we must stop worrying about how God intends to work our issues and be secure that it's going to be better than how we expected it to be in the end!

I'm reminded of Proverbs 3:5

"Trust in and rely confidently on the LORD with all your

heart And do not rely on your own insight or understanding."

Life doesn't come with a manual or crystal ball. Unfortunately right? Lol....However we have something more precise. When we don't understand what is going on in our lives we can put our lives in the God's hands. It's a secure place. A place of peace in the midst of a storm. Interestingly enough, no one can do it for you. It's a place only you can go to yourself. Beloved we must believe He is working it out for our good. And when this trial is over with your marriage, finances, health, business, home, or eye situation like mine, we will understand, with the help of the Holy Spirit, God's wisdom and knowledge is amazing!

So Trust God No Matter What! I have to remind myself daily during this eye injury journey. Living on your savings account is no fun! But I thank God in his wisdom and my obedience while I was working I saved. However, I know it won't sustain us forever. God knows when to step in at the right time and turn things around. Jesus took 2 loaves and 5 fish and fed 5,000 people. With leftovers! He's the same yesterday, today, and forever. Remember, He knows and sees all. We are not alone.

The direction you and I desperately want to travel, God may instruct that it may not be time just yet. Or now is the time! Or the person you are praying for may need a little growing first. Or you just need to slow down and rest a bit. Whatever it is, God knows best. God will remain faithful knowing He will bless us just when we put it all in His hands, but first we must trust God's plan.

I urge you today to trust Him even when you can't trace Him. Declare you will trust Him and let every anxiety, & worry go and surrender it all to His will. That's what I'm doing.

NOTES

DAY #17

The God Of Grace

◆ ◆ ◆

Have you ever faced a season where you don't know where to go? Your current situation has dried up? Lost a job, lost a home, health turns south for you or a loved one, lost finances, lost passion for your occupation, lost your vision (physically like me or spiritually) or even lost a loved one? Beloved you are not alone. These are times where our faith gets put on trial. Nobody is immune. It's a part of life and a part of everyone's journey. In these times of testing and uncertainty we need our Papa or Daddy God the most!

> *Simply Ask Him To Lead You! He stands outside of time. He had the solution to your problem before you were even born.*

It was laid on my heart today to ask God for His guidance and allow Him to lead me to the next steps in my career. Should I return to be a great Endodontist and business owner and boss. Or is there something else bigger and better? It's day #17 of my eye injury and God is doing an amazing work in the background. I don't know exactly what he's doing but I know it's going to be awesome!

Sometimes in life, we have an idea of how we want our lives to unfold, but God already knows what is in our future. See when I was young about 6 years old, I wanted to be a clown. Do you remember the Bozo Show out of Chicago? Well I wanted to have fun and make people laugh. Then as I got older in middle school I wanted to be a reporter. Why? My mom said I asked a lot of questions, I was nosy, and my teachers said I talked too much! Then I wanted to play baseball for the Atlanta Braves. Finally, I had a mentor who was a dentist in high school. A God moment. He exposed me to other careers in healthcare however I decided to become a dentist. We attended the same college and dental school without even planning it! I eventually went back to my hometown and worked for him as a dentist. Then that well dried up so to speak. I had a friend that was in a root canal residency program in Fort Lauderdale at NOVA. I went to visit to escape my reality and go on vacation. He tricked me to going to the dental school to watch him perform a root canal under a microscope. I got hooked. I applied to the program. I got denied acceptance. Then by the grace of God I got a call back for a spot. I was the 5th resident and they usually only took four. 5 is the number of Grace! It's been almost 20 years now!

Jeremiah 29:11-12 reminds us, God already has a plan for our lives. From the foundation of the world he had good things in store for us. We simply need to ask Him to reveal it to us, get on board and trust Him to be our source and light! His plans may change for us but it will always lead us into greener pastures. This day #17 of my eye injury didn't catch God by surprise. He's not wondering oh my God (no pun intended) what are we going to do now Jesus and The Holy Spirit. Rico is injured. His bills are mounting. His savings is draining. He represents me on earth. We are worried! No no non...it's just the opposite. He's sitting back with his crews smiling. Saying I can't wait until the world sees how I'm going to bring him out of this. Like a good parent who bought all kinds of stuff for Christmas and can't wait to see their faces unwrap the gifts on Christmas Day!

So if you are lost today and don't know what to do or where to go. Ask God for direction. He loves to hear from you. He treats you like you are his only child. You are the apple of his eyes. The focus of his affection! He will give you grace to finish your race!

NOTES

DAY #18

God Is Up To Something

◆ ◆ ◆

Are you facing a drought in an area of your life? Perhaps in your marriage, finances, business, home, or health. Does it feel as if God has left you? Just because it looks like nothing doesn't mean God isn't up to something!

In 1 Kings 18:43-44 there was a famine in the land due to a drought. Elijah who was a prophet, believed God would end the drought therefore, he continued to pray for rain. I bet people thought he was crazy because he kept believing when it really looked like a dead situation. However, he trusted God would stay faithful to His promise. That's where I am at today dealing with my eye situation. I'm believing my drought will end soon. God will restore my sight even better than before the accident, my finances better, my health better, my marriage better, my practice better, my life better!

When you are going through a drought season persistence & prayer is key!

Are we willing to be persistent and continue to pray in a land of drought? Elijah was not only persistent but he did not take "no" for an answer. Each time his servant came back to report there was no sign of rain, he instructed him to go back a total of seven times before there was even a small sign of cloud. Seven is the number of perfection and completion. See Jesus is our number seven! He came so we can have life and life more abundantly in other words a full and complete life.

Many times in life we give up too easily – when the doctor says "no," when the loan doesn't go through, when you've failed an exam, an eye injury jeopardizing your career, when we have one bad day, an opportunity falls through or our kids are acting crazy we want to throw in the towel! However, we must realize God is listening to every one of our prayers and He's a very present help. **<u>Don't ever stop praying.</u>** Your prayers are providing a constant and powerful breakthrough. God sent Elijah a small sign – a cloud the size of a man's hand and soon after there was a heavy rain! Although you may not see huge progress today, God is forming small clouds on your behalf. I believe my sight has improved even just a little…maybe 1%. I'm thankful for that even before the surgery scheduled next week. Who knows a miracle can happen the day before my surgery and I'm fully recovered! I'm not giving up hope!

So is there an area in your life you have given up? In your vision spiritually or physically, finances, health, marriage, or business? Beloved! You are just another day away from victory! Celebrate your small victories! Small victories like a cloud the size of a man's hand will certain to bring about a big downpour of blessings in the future. Stand strong knowing God is forming clouds for you because of Jesus finished work in you! Read that again out loud. A downpour is surely coming your way if you don't give up believing and speaking your faith into the atmosphere!

<u>NOTES</u>

DAY #19

God Is Present

◆ ◆ ◆

Yesterday, I spoke to a crowd of almost 100 dentist at the Waldorf Astoria in Atlanta. It was the first time I've spoken since my eye incident. It was a 3-hour lecture and I wasn't sure if I was going to be able to do it using only one eye. Well the crowd was "Edutained"! It was another amazing experience. At the end I told them my eye injury story. They asked how are you staying so positive? I said my faith has grown strong during this season. When I finished lecturing, there was an Asian dentist that came up to me. I didn't know him at all. He said Dr. Short you did an amazing lecture and thank you. But can I do something for you? I said sure. He said I am not just a dentist, I'm a pastor. I felt your faith on display while you lectured. I'm led by the spirit of God to pray for you. I said right here in front of everybody? He said if you want. I said let's do it. Let me tell you....This guy prayed such an amazing prayer over my eye and my life that I felt God was reincarnated into this person whom I've never met or seen before like an angel! It was truly the highlight of my experience yesterday. He said he is a pastor and dentist in a small town called Auburn Georgia. I'm from Georgia and never heard of that place...lol. God is Good!

NOTES

DAY #20

He Has Started A Good Work

◆ ◆ ◆

We have been created and designed for God's use. We were created in his image and likeness. However, in this journey of life we will still encounter challenges and obstacles that seem contrary to that previous statement. I call them transitional moments.

Transitional moments can be very scary. They're not in your daily planner and often not very convenient. It can happen in the blink of an eye leaving you wondering what am I going to do now? Kinda like my eye injury. At the blink of an eye, literally, while going down a water slide on vacation with my family, my right thumb punctured my left eye leading me to day #20 and can't practice the skill in which I love. Furthermore, with the injury I don't have income but the expenses are continuing. So what am I to do? Trust God! See I'm fully convinced that God who began this glorious work in me will faithfully continue the process of maturing me and will put his finishing touches on me and bring me out better than before (Philippians 1:6). He has an awesome track record of doing that...look at Abraham, Moses, Joseph, Joshua, Jesus, Paul, etc. All these great men of faith encountered adversity which lead them to transitional moments that ultimately lead them into their destiny!

Are you facing a tough time now in your finances, on your job, in your church, in your health? ***This could be a transitional moment.*** See these moments are where miracles are birthed. These moments are where millionaires are made. Don't be afraid of this transitional moment. Embrace it! Ask God to give you spiritual eyes to see and a tender heart to trust. I'm not saying it will be easy. But I'm saying it will be worth it. Since this eye injury I've been awake many nights just wondering what I am going to do. Will I lose everything I worked so hard for? Will my practice survive? Will me and my family enjoy our new home we worked so hard to obtain? Using my spiritual eyes I can hear God say, Relax…it's going to end better than you think!

Ephesians 2:10 says We are His workmanship created in Christ Jesus unto good works. God desires for us to walk in his fullness and I order to be able to do that our soul and body must be in good shape. If it's not, then we just simply as Him to help us and believe that He will. Just like I'm believing for my eye to be healed, I'm asking God while he's fixing that fix anything else in there that's wrong. Like a mechanic going in to fix your engine, if there's anything else to be fixed while it's open fix it too!

Today, perhaps like me you are in a transitional moment. Let me encourage you it's going to be amazing on the other side! Start embracing it. Listen to your heart, ask God how your life can be used to give Him praise. This doesn't mean you're going to live a broke life that's dull. No! It's quite the opposite. It will be enriched and full and adventurous. God I'm ready for whatever you have in store for me and my family. Beloved, cease to live a self-fulfilled life playing it safe life, and let God begin to use you for His purpose. Then you will begin to really really live.

NOTES

DAY #21

Temporary Tears

◆ ◆ ◆

Throughout life we will encounter various challenges and yes even lose some things. People that say they love you may turn their backs on you. It could be a close friend, a mentor, a parent, or even a spouse. However, there is someone who said they will never turn their back on you. God promises in Psalms 27:10 if your mother or father forsakes you, He will remain. In other words your tears of betrayal will be temporary when you put your heart in his hands. In His Word, it tells us depend on no one, but stand and lean on God alone. Not your parents, your spouse, not referring dentist for those who are specialist, not your children, but only God.

> *"It is better to trust in the Lord than to put confidence in man"* (Psalm 118:8 KJV).

It's day #21 and to be honest I still can't wrap my mind around this eye injury. But it doesn't matter because my heart is wrapped around the faithfulness of Jesus. See, I understand God is more interested in developing us in the journey versus just arriving at the destination. Get that. Development produces faith. Faith is what move mountains.

Throughout life, we may lose a loved one, a career, a ministry, a spouse, a practice, a health situation turns south, or a relationship may come to a sudden end, and we may find ourselves stuck in the moment. Remember it's just a moment. Not a lifetime. Be determined, no matter what, that you will depend on God during this difficult period in your life. Know your tears are only temporary and there will be a time when you will not have to cry anymore. Did you know God collects all your tears and place them in a bottle? Read Psalms 58:8. This is significant! That's how much he's involved in your everyday life. God loves giving us beauty for ashes and turning our sorrows into joy (Isaiah 61:3).

I love Corinthians 4:17 MSG

> *"So we're not giving up. How could we! Even though on the outside it often looks like things are falling apart on us, on the inside, where God is making new life, not a day goes by without his unfolding grace. These hard times are small potatoes compared to the coming good times; the lavish celebration prepared for us. There's far more here than meets the eye. The things we see now are here today, gone tomorrow. But the things we can't see now will last forever."*

Beloved, whatever is causing you tears it's just temporary. If you are still alive, God has something wonderful and amazing for your future. He only gives purpose to living things. So today stop dwelling on what's in your past. It's dead. Bury it. Move forward. God desires for you to let go of your past and grasp your future by following Him. Jesus says in Luke 9, "Follow me!"....." Let the dead bury the dead." Why? Because you are so alive in Him! You have not seen your best days!

So let me encourage you to let go and live again. This eye injury journey has been scary and fascinating to say the least. God has provided for me, my family, my home, and my business every step of the way. It's going on 2 months now with no income and yet we are still standing by the Grace of God. See I can't let this thing get me down. I'm believing for doors to supernaturally open for more favor to shine on me and my family.

I'm believing this for you too. Perhaps you've lost a loved one, a business, a dream, a part of your body, and feel all hope is lost. You feel there is a part of you that died. But, let me tell you we have someone in the resurrection business. He can resurrect anything that you lost or is dead in your life. His name is Jesus Christ. In the middle of your crisis now he's there! Just ask Him to bring this dead part of your life back. Whenever he does it, it will always be better in quantity and quality. Go back and read Jesus first miracle when he turned water into wine. Not just wine but fine wine, way more than they could drink, with no price tag! He is the Lilly of your valley. He is your bright and morning star in darkness. God wants to replace all your sorrow with unspeakable joy. Let go of the temporary tears and grasp the permanent cheers. Know God is doing a new thing in your life right now. He is taking everything in your past and turning them around for your good (Romans 8:28).

Begin to trust Him and Him alone. I pray you ask God today to remove any dependence on people or things or whatever you lost in the past. Ask God to fill you with His presence and do a new thing! That's where his fullness, joy, and treasures forevermore are located!

IN THE EYE OF A STORM

NOTES

DAY #22

Full Speed Ahead

◆ ◆ ◆

For such a long time, I thought giving God my Sunday was enough. I didn't want Him messing with my rest of the week. Those other days I wanted to have fun and didn't want a "chaperone". If I wanted to have fun, or let's be honest sin a little, I didn't want Him to see me or it. I thought since I prayed on occasion, attended church decently, and would attempt to do what is right most of the time, that was enough for God. He would give me my smiley face or star sticker for the week like in kindergarten.

Well as I matured, that's not what I realized God is after. The reality is, God wants all of our lives, not just a part of it. He's not a part-time God. He never gets tired of us. He never gets anxious for us. He never grows weary with us. He's really a good good Father who's always with us, protects us, rejoices over us with joy, don't mention our past sins, enjoys laughter with us and singing over us! He has an amazing sense of humor as well. I love what Zephaniah 3:17 says

"The LORD your God is in your midst, A Warrior who

saves. He will rejoice over you with singing; He will make no mention of your past sins, He will rejoice over you with shouts of joy."

This is all made possible by Jesus finished work on the cross. He satisfied all the requirements of the law so we can live at peace with God perpetually.

You may be saying....Dr. Short what does it mean to give God your all? It means to simply trust the finished work of Jesus on your behalf and welcome him into every area of your life. Even in your current situation. I'm trusting him in this eye injury journey on day #22. Boy do I miss doing pain free root canals and making people feel better! That is one of my gifts and calling. However, I know that God can equip us with more than one gift and calling. Maybe he's doing a new thing and refining what's already inside of me and you too for that matter.

Most folks don't like change. They like dollars!...lol. No just kidding. One of the most frustrating things in life is to expect everything to say the same. That's not reality. That's not living. Life changes fast with or without you. There's no need to be afraid of change if you have the one person who doesn't. That person is Jesus. He's the same yesterday, today, and forever. That's why I haven't gone nuts after this eye injury after 22 days. I've learned in times of uncertainty surrender your life to the one who knows all things and can turn any impossibility into many possibilities.

When you decide to give God your all, I must admit it can be scary and intimidating. Is God going to go through all my stuff? Is he going to find all the skeletons in my closet? Well the good news is he was with you when you were making the skeletons and while you were cramming them in your closet! Oh wait a minute. A rib just fell out while you were listening to me...Lol...You know what really amazes me? Being open and honest with him. Every time I do that and let go of something,

He gives me a peace about it, pats me on my back, and says we're in this together! Then he restores and resurrects what I gave to him pressed down, shaken together, and running over! Remember he said in his word he will never leave nor forsake us. In fact the word used was an emphatic never, ever, ever!

In your time of trouble, you have to trust that God knows what is best for you. My eye injury didn't come as a surprise to him. Just like a loved one you lost, a spouse that walked out on you, a business that didn't make it, or a dream that hasn't manifested yet. He has a plan. The plan is well thought out and full proof. You just have to trust he has your best interest in mind. If something is not working in your life, give it up to Him. When you surrender and align your plans with His, it may hurt for a moment, but God will eventually turn your sadness into joy and give you strength during the storm. You will get to a place and wonder, why didn't I trust God in the first place?

This happens at the end of the journey when you're picking up all the buried treasure. Beloved, God will give you more than your heart could have ever imagined. I've experienced it before and now believing for it once again...Full Speed Ahead! I'm believing that for me and you too at the end of this chapter of your life journey. You will look back and see only goodness and mercy following you once again!

NOTES

DAY #23

You Have The Creator Inside Of You

◆ ◆ ◆

In Genesis 1:1 God created. He made something from nothing. Read that again.
God. Created.
Or to explain it with a little more detail: God did something, then bang that something responded into form!
God is creative. And because we are made in His image and likeness, We are creative too!

You may be in a period of change like me, of uncertainty, of wondering what is next. It's day #23 of my eye injury and still no change. However, I feel a deep call to be faithful to God in the process. Everyone in the Bible who did something great had to go through a process. Just to name a few:

* Abraham - God told him he would be the father of all nations without any child yet. Had to wait until almost 100 years old finally bang it happened!

* Noah - Built an ark when there was no sign of rain and people said he was crazy. When it started to rain him and his family

were saved.

* Joseph - Thrown in a pit, sold as a slave, went to the palace, thrown in jail for 14 years for something he didn't do, had favor in jail, then back to the palace as prime minister!

* Peter - Denied Jesus 3 times with cursing and swearing yet Jesus said upon Peter (his revelation of Christ) is what the church will be built on.

* Paul - Originally threw Christians in jail and assisted in murdering them yet got a revelation of Jesus and wrote 2/3 of the New Testament.

Now is the time to remember the first thing you know about God, and the first thing you know about yourself. You were created to be creative and thrive in life! So even though you may have a setback in life - lost a home, lost sight in one eye, a broken relationship, failing business, lost hearing, or the ability to walk or drive or work, lost a marriage, drowning in debt, or whatever! I want to encourage you as I encourage myself that we have a wonderful treasure in earthen vessels. His name is Jesus. Not only he can heal and mend your situation he can resurrect it into new life! In fact, He Is The Resurrection and Life and He lives inside of us!

In John 11:25 Jesus said,

> *"I AM the resurrection and the life."*

As you keep your faith flowing and your eyes on Jesus and off the situation, you will see new life come out of dust, wonderful ideas become reality, and broken and disconnected things become fresh and whole.

PRAY THIS WITH ME TODAY:

God of all creation, thank You for the gift of how You made me, unique from every other person born. No one has my same fingerprints or teeth for that matter. Thank You for the gift of life. Where there is life there is Hope. Where there is Hope there is Purpose. Where there is Purpose you have a Plan. That Plan is ALWAYS Good. As I breathe in I am reminded that it is Your breath in my lungs and your creativity is in me that gives me life. As I breathe out and speak about you to others, I am reminded that I also get to bring life to others. Thank You for sending Jesus to show us your heart for mankind. I am loved deeply by you and there is no good thing you will withhold from me. I will trust in the Holy Spirit to be my inner compass and guide through this unforeseen journey of life filled with hills and valleys. He will guide me into peace and truth. For He also knows where all the buried treasure is located in me and in the earth. Father, I thank you that I'm loved not for obeying religious rules or making all the right decisions but simply because I am Your creation and I find myself located in Jesus.

NOTES

DAY #24

◆ ◆ ◆

Joy & Pain

You've probably heard the song by Rob Base "Joyyyy....Painnnn....Sunshine....and Rain..." You probably heard some religious person say, "**Count It All Joy When Facing Pain!" And you are like this person got to be smoking crack or something! LOL. How can joy and pain coexist?**

This verse in the book of James is often quoted to imply that in the midst of trials, we need to be happy and "have a coke and a smile." That is not what James intends here. As Christians, or humans for that matter, we will have to face adversity in this life however we don't have to be happy about it. Happiness is not what James is writing about. Joy is what James is writing about! What's the difference? Happiness is a feeling based on external circumstances and subject to change like the weather or your bank account. Joy is an internal fact based on confidence in Jesus finished work and God's deep unconditional love for us. Joy is constant and consistent because it's based on God's Word. The Bible says everything in this world will change but God's Word will remain the same. That's good news!

You may be thinking so Dr. Short....happiness isn't a gift from God? Happiness is indeed a gift from God, but happiness will not sustain us through the difficulties that come from living in a fallen world. My dad asked who is non-believer asked if God is good and you are a good person why did He let something like this eye accident happen to you? That's a rhetorical life question. Sometimes we don't know the answer. There was nothing to be happy about when I had my eye injury and its day #24 and my situation hasn't changed but there is something I know inside. I know that the joy of the Lord is my strength and shield (Psalms 28:7). He will protect me and get me through this eye injury journey. The other side of this journey will produce a great testimony to leave as a legacy for others to follow!

There are tv channels now that rebroadcasts old sports games and movies. Why would someone watch when they already know how it ends? That is precisely why they watch! They know how it ends. It gives them a sense of peace and comfort.
That's the channel Jesus wants us to fix our eyes on! Get that! We are in a fixed fight with Jesus on our side. That's good news! We know how Jesus' story ends. Therefore yours will end in the same way...victorious! That is the joy that James the brother of Jesus writes about to his congregation who were flagging in their faith. We know that we are so loved by a Father that he sent His one and only Son to redeem us by dying on a cross. So you may be facing a trial in your health, marriage, finances, church, relationships, on your job, with an addiction, whatever. Trials will come to the best of the best and worst of the worst. **<u>Trials produces pain and it will produce joy.</u>** But be of good cheer because you know how your story ends! Jesus said be of good cheer because in me you will have peace, I have overcome the world (John 16:33).

My Prayer Today:
Father, I pray that when the fallen world brings trials that your Holy Spirit will help us to fix our eyes on Jesus. He is the only an-

chor in this world. He is the living hope that sustains us, not our own skills, spiritual advisor, or parents. Because God is a loving Father, He allows trials to teach us that Christ and His sacrifice is our only hope that produces incredible joy. This world isn't our home. We are just passing through. Heaven is the perfect place where there is no pain, no sorrow, and no trials. Father continue to point us repeatedly to the cross and Jesus finished work because it is where we will see our victory in this world! Amen.

DR RICO D SHORT

NOTES

DAY #25

God Hears Us

◆ ◆ ◆

Sometimes we find ourselves in situations where we feel stuck. No Vision. Blurred Vision (like my eye). No hope. Life seems a bit stale. We wonder does God care. Is he listening to our prayer? The answer is YES!

Do you remember as a child, you always wanted to be an adult? You wanted to drive. You wanted to have no curfew. You wanted to party all night long. Well I guess it's only me because I don't see you shaking your head or raising your hand. Then bam, overnight you become an adult. Now it isn't as fun as you thought. More responsibilities and more challenges get thrown our way. Adjusting to a new job, heck finding a job, starting a business from scratch like me, running a business and managing staff, dealing with an eye injury like me or any health issue while helping to raise two teenage girls can be a daunting task…all this change can be at times almost too much to bear!

Beloved, we don't have to do this alone. I know you may be thinking, well Dr. Short you are a doctor, you have a wife, you have money, etc. let me tell you something, all of those ways you are thinking I have it "all together" doesn't exempt me or anyone else from life problems. Fortunately, as a follower of Christ, I know where all my success came from and where my source of answers to all of life's problems are located.

Life gets busy for all of us and can be very difficult at times. More money will not solve all your problems just like a lack of money won't. Life can be very stressful trying to manage it all on your own. It's designed like that on purpose by our creator. We're designed to depend on the creator of the universe in order to live a successful and purposeful life. This happens when we speak to God about any and everything. The religious term is called praying. I call it conversing. We supposed to converse with God and seek His guidance, no matter if everything is going well or the wheels are falling off! God knows us through and through. He wired us according to His divine plan and desires an intimate relationship with us. He wants us to ask Him for stuff!

You may be asking so why do we have to ask for what He's already aware of? See God isn't like a genie that will give you 3 wishes or like Dr. Spock who wants to read your mind. No. He's a good father that desires relationship with his children. Can you imagine if your child only comes to you when they need money? How would that make you feel? Especially as a good parent you know they need much more than that to be successful in this world. You know they will have challenges, fear, pain, and will face disappointments. God knows that too and He cares about our pain and trials we will face in this life.

First Thessalonians tells us to pray without ceasing (5:17). Does that mean literally to recite The Lord's Prayer 24/7 like a broken record? Of course not. I like the passion version. It says

> *"Let joy be your continual feast. Make your life a prayer. And in the midst of everything be always giving thanks, for this is God's perfect plan for you in Christ Jesus."*

Joy and Thanksgiving is the key. If you can find joy in whatever situation you encounter, be thankful! It will give you more depth and understanding of the heart of God in the situation. Furthermore, as you simply talk to God and invite him into every aspect of your life, your life begins to beautifully unfold to become one big prayer! Nothing to memorize or to recite. God says he will write everything on our heart in Jeremiah 31:33.

Because of Jesus finished work we are as loved and forgiven as Jesus in the eyes of God. Yes! As forgiven children of God, we get the opportunity to hold an open line of communication between us and the Creator of the universe. How cool is that! But do you know what causes static in the prayer line of communication? It's Stress which creates Distractions which creates Unbelief that waters down our Faith & Hope.

So how do we overcome this static in our prayer line? Devote a special time with God every day. Without any distractions. God desires intimacy with you and He will hear you! James 5:16 states the earnest and heartfelt prayer of a Believer makes tremendous power available and will rearrange or turn the situation around for good! Don't ever neglect the power of prayer even if you don't see or feel something happening. As His children, we are to remember to pray for ourselves and for one another and that He holds our lives in His hands. There ain't no other hands to be in besides his and maybe AllState! Lol...

Unfortunately as humans and as men especially, we feel we can do everything on our own. This is creates prideful behavior and ungodly thoughts. Sound familiar? Adam and Eve thought the same thing and really got us in the mess we are in today. However Jesus, in his mercy and grace, stepped out of heaven and put an earth suit on. He undid what Adam and Eve did in the garden and now our daddy God can't wait to hear from us every day! There is no part of our life that's too small or too big for our

Daddy God to be interested in! When we pray and communicate with Him, we're recognizing His power and sovereignty over all things. Our problems will slowly and surely melt away as we place Him in the center.

My Prayer Today:
Daddy God, Papa, forgive me for not coming to You with all my cares and requests. You sent Jesus to be the open door straight to the throne room of Grace. I can now come boldly and bring everything to you even in the midst of my sins. You are ready to hear about my hurt, my pain, my lost, and my frustration. You love me the exact same as you love Jesus and are faithful not only to hear my prayers but answer them as well. Overwhelm me with Your presence and peace today and guide me in following Your will during all seasons of life. In Jesus name. Amen.

NOTES

DAY #26

The Winds of Change

◆ ◆ ◆

Do you like change? For the most part none of us do! However change is necessary and unavoidable. God created life to change and contain various seasons. It can be scary yet at the same time very beautiful. In life, winds create change.

So how does wind form? **Wind** comes from atmospheric **changes**: **changes** in temperature and pressure makes the air move around the surface of the earth. All of which **is** triggered by the sun.

Likewise we have changes in our life that can disrupt our "atmosphere" like losing a job, our finances goes south, we have to relocate, deal with a health issue, an eye injury, etc. All of this creates a pressure inside of us and all around us. Sometimes it's triggered by the S-O-N to increase our faith. You may be saying Dr. Short you've gone too far. Well let me remind you of this story in Mark chapter 3.

Earlier that day, Jesus fed 5000 men not including the women and children with a Captain D's 2-piece fish and chips snack kid's meal. This was about 20,000 people that was fed that would have costed a half of a year's wages with a little boy's lunch. What a Miracle! It was a mountaintop experience! The disciples were CRUNK! They wanted to stay with Jesus, but He sent them away immediately… out into a boat…after midnight…purposefully…with a storm approaching! That's Jesus? Really? That's not cool?…you are thinking WHAT!

Have you ever wondered why He did that? Why would Jesus who's full of love and compassion let us face such trials, painful, and difficult circumstances? Does He really love us? The disciples previously asked, "Teacher, do you not care that we are going to die?" You've may have asked that question before or perhaps now as you are reading this. Jesus I love you, I go to church, I treat folks right, I tithe, I pray, I fast…blah blah blah. Yet these things don't immune you from the challenges of life.

Now let me get back to the story…it was dark, the disciples were in the boat in the middle of the sea, and Jesus was alone on the land. Sometimes in life when you face challenges it will often feel dark, isolated, and left alone. Many times it can come right off the heels of a major victory or miracle. But Jesus eyes are still on you and your current situation.

> *"Jesus seeing the disciples straining at the oars, because the wind was against them, at about the fourth watch of the night (3:00-6:00 a.m.) He came to them, walking on the sea. And acted as if He intended to pass by them. For they all saw Him and were shaken and terrified." (Mark 6:48-49)*

Let me unpack this a little more. Jesus will never ever take his eyes off you. He may wait to show up at your darkest hour which is right before sunrise. You may feel as if He doesn't understand. Like He's passing you by. Like the song Passin' Me By from Pharcyde…..lol. In addition, when they saw Him walking on the water I know they cursed! I would have….Like Oh…#@#$$!..it's a ghost. That's my interpretation….lol. As the story goes He immediately spoke with them and said,

> *"Take courage! It is I (I AM)! Stop being afraid."* (Mark 6:50)

I love this part. Jesus will confront you face to face and say STOP BEING AFRAID! Also He says, "I Am". This term was first used in Genesis as another name for God. Jesus is whatever you need:

*   I am the **Bread of Life** (John 6:35) - If you hunger after righteousness

*   I am the **Light of the World** (John 8:12) - If you are in darkness

*   I am the **Door** (John 10:9) - If you can't find your way out of your situation

*   I am the **Good Shepherd** (John 10:11,14) - If you need protection & guidance

*   I am the **Resurrection and the Life** (John 11:25) - If something's dead in your life

-       I am the **Way and the Truth and the Life** (John 14:6) - If you're lost

-       I am the **Vine** (John 15:1,5) - If you want to live an abundant fruitful life

What situation are you facing right now and are afraid? Is it bullying? Are you too fat? Too skinny? Too poor? Too rich? In life we will all be afraid of something and the wind of change will affect us but when we put Jesus in our boat He calms everything down!

> *"Then He got into the boat with them, and the wind ceased as if exhausted by its own activity, and they were completely overwhelmed, because they had not understood the miracle of the loaves how it revealed the power and deity of Jesus." (Mark 6:51).*

Jesus saved the disciples that night. And He is always faithful to save us, too. But why does He allow us to suffer? And why can He seem so far away when we are crying out to Him? Does it mean that we are out of God's will? I don't think so. Check this out, Jesus made them get in the boat! He wanted them to be there! This blew me away when I saw this. Verse 52 says,

> *"...for they [the disciples] did not understand about the loaves, but their hearts were hardened."*

God is the only one who really knows our hearts! Could the disciples been groupies for Jesus? Enjoying the fame, the status, etc. but really didn't understand the reason behind it all? Even just for this moment? At times our faith will be put to the test. This is not to hurt us but to allow us to draw nearer to our Daddy God. He will continue to give us test after test after test. There are no grades. Just pass or retake. God knows we cannot learn ALL of the lessons when times are good. In fact, I believe we learn more in the valleys than the hills.

Just remember whatever wind of change is blowing your way, embrace it and keep your eyes on Jesus. All works all things together for our good (Romans 8:28), even in experiences we would never choose for ourselves like my eye injury journey. Jesus has now calmed my boat emotionally and spiritually. Now I'm just waiting for the healing of my eye naturally or supernaturally. I will see again. I will practice again. My finances will be restored again. My business will be restored again.

My Prayer Today....
Daddy God, Thank You for being with us in the easy things and hard things. Thank You for sending Jesus and loving us so much that You, too, suffered for our good with Jesus on the cross. Your hands and feet were pierced as well. Please help us to respond to every circumstance of life the way You want us to. Counting it all JOY! We can only do that by the help of the Holy Spirit inside of us. Continue to Make us more like You. We love You. Amen.

NOTES

DAY #27

When Your Brook Dries Up

◆ ◆ ◆

Humans tend to be a creature of habit. We always want to find a comfortable place in life and stay there. Staying at the same job, relationship, church, home etc. for 20 + years with no desire to change.

There is nothing inherently wrong with that. However, there are times when God stop his blessings in that location. That brook has dried up. Elijah experienced that in 1 Kings 17. Elijah was a prophet of God. GOD told Elijah to go hide out at the Kerith Ravine. A ravine is a deep, narrow gorge with steep sides. A secluded place of comfort for Elijah and maybe you are in that place now in your job or hometown. God gave him fresh water to drink from the brook in the ravine and ordered the ravens to feed him breakfast, lunch, and dinner. Man that's a plush lifestyle. However, there was a drought and eventually the brook dried up. We don't know the time frame. It could have been 7 days, 7 months, or 7 years.

I don't know if you've ever had a brook dry up on you. It's not cool. It's scary, uncomfortable, and nerve racking. With my eye injury that's how I felt for some time. I can't practice. It's been 40 days with no income. My practice seems to be drying up. And using one eye to function is difficult. Has my brook dried up? Is it time for a change? Change in career? Change in location? Change in lifestyle? God knows I'm not ready to cash in on all my hard work and success in the sweet spot of my career at 45 years old of being a successful Endodontist for 20 years. Or maybe it's just a season I'm in. God is trying to grow me and stretch my faith. I believe God has something bigger and better on the other side of this eye injury journey!

Do you feel your brook has dried up? Don't worry! God has a trillion ways to bless us. Yes He was supplying our needs in one way, but then He stopped. He doesn't always tell us why and many times it's nothing you did or didn't do. It's just time to move on.

Oftentimes, He'll give us a signal in the middle of the dry season. I've experienced this before. I was a general dentist in 1999 practicing in my hometown of Columbus Georgia. Living with my mom, saving money, and working with my mentor who was a very successful dentist. After a year of working there, things started going awry. The brook started drying up. I was scared and frustrated at the same time. I went to visit a good friend who was in an Endodontic residency program at Nova Southeastern University in Ft. Lauderdale to get some rest and relaxation. I was looking forward to South Beach not any teeth! He tricked me to helping him assist performing a root canal using a microscope. I thought it was very interesting but not enough to get excited over. My situation was dry back home. He encouraged me to apply to the program. I did nonchalantly. I got accepted. And the rest is history!

God was telling me at the time "It's time to move on. I've got something new for you to do." I didn't see it or understand it. Losing your brook can be frustrating and scary. You were comfortable. You were at home. Things were just beginning to come together. You were getting good at doing what you were doing.....(I was able to pull a tooth like a magician would pull a rabbit out of a hat...Pain Free without them even knowing)You were in a familiar place. You were making plans to build something great near your brook so that you could stay there forever. Then...surprise! God allowed the brook to dry up. That's God saying...I have bigger plans for you....saddle up we are getting ready to ride again!

I think God allows our brook to dry up because we can get stale there. No growth. No challenge. When we get comfortable, we stop depending on him or our impact on our environment has declined. By drying up the brook, He forces us to search out His provision in another place. What an awesome opportunity! The Word of God says we go from glory to glory. There should always be an upward movement in the life of a Believer.

> *Then GOD spoke to him: "Get up and go to Zarephath in Sidon and live there. I've instructed a woman who lives there, a widow, to feed you." (1 Kings 17:2-9 MSG)*

What if Elijah had never left the brook? He wouldn't have been able to help the widow and her son. He would not have won the victory against Ahab's prophets. He would not have been able to pass the mantle to his mentee Elisha.

Likewise with you. Somebody needs what you have. They are waiting on you to move. You are in their dream home and someone else is in yours. That's what happened to us last year! You need someone to help you get to your dream job and vice versa. Someone needs you to mentor them and you need one for your next assignment.

Let me encourage you. Don't complain when God dries up your brook. It's a divine set up! It's okay to be sad and feel uncomfortable for a short time. That's normal. That's human. However, sooner or later, our faith kicks in gear and we depend on God the most. Faith is the currency of heaven that moves the hand of God towards a miracle for you. Read that again! So the sooner we get up and get moving, the sooner God can show us our next assignment. It will be filled with more than you can ever ask, imagine, or think possible!

My Prayer...
Lord, help me to trust You when my brook dries up. I know you are a good Father and always have my best interest in mind. Give me Your Holy Spirit to guide me to my next destination you have planned for me. I know it will be a place flowing with milk and honey..my promised land. And when I make it there, use me as a vessel to help others get to theirs as well. In Jesus Name. Amen.

NOTES

DAY #28

Being Stable As The World Turns

◆ ◆ ◆

I don't watch much tv but I remember as a kid watching a soap opera with my grandmother called "As The World Turns". The show featured drama, drama, and more drama involving the personal and professional lives of doctors and lawyers throughout its run for 54 years. Some of it was real and some of it was fantasy. But it was very hard to decipher the difference. There were many emotional roller coasters on the show just like in real life. This happened even amongst the elite and professional just like the average person.

Many of us struggle to accept the current circumstances we cannot change. Whether it's an eye injury like mine, or perhaps laid off from a job, a recent divorce, a child having psycho-social issues trying to fit in, or financial setbacks. We can make a decision to camp out there or continue to move forward in life.

Change is never easy. But it is unavoidable "as the world turns". And sometimes you may ask "Why is this happening to me? When will this be over? Does God loved me? I don't feel loved and this is not fair!" Yet, the Bible says Jesus learned obedience through what He suffered in Hebrews 5:8.

Let me unpack this verse. The word often translated as obedience is the word, upoakuo, which means under the influence of hearing, or active hearing from above. Jesus continued to hear from above when things got really stressful. That's what we need to do as well dealing with change. When we learn to "lean" upon God's love it simplifies your 'emotional hearing' so that your thoughts are in harmony with Jesus thoughts and his finished work. He's already your accomplished your righteousness, joy, and peace!

It really is as basic as de-cluttering your mind in the daily grind of life. When faced with situations that bring negative emotions, anxiety, a sense of shame or limitation ask yourself if what you are thinking is in accordance with the state, atmosphere, and personality of heaven. Think about that! As you transform your thinking, you actually 'distance yourself from the effect' of those negative emotions and thought patterns. This brings you peace and joy in the midst of chaos. Will this be easy? Wil this be a one-time event? No! This will take practice over and over again. And trust me you will have plenty of opportunities to practice daily.

As I progress through Day #28 of my eye injury, I must stay focused on the current moment. I can't let my mind wonder about tomorrow. I must be stable as the world turns. So it is with you with whatever issue you are dealing with. Keep your eyes on Jesus and off anything negative. Speak your faith and future into the atmosphere. It has plenty of ears and your angels love to listen to your requests. Until then sometimes the Lord may not change our circumstances right away. But he's in the process of changing us as the world turns to be more like Jesus. Trust that His plan is greater than anything we can imagine, ask, or think!

My Prayer...
Daddy God, teach us what it means to maintain the proper attitude in the process of change. Thank You for sending Jesus to be

our greatest example of this. Jesus understands our issues perfectly because he came down from heaven and put an earth suit on. You became one of us in Christ. Help us to cling to You...the One that never changes. Help us to be stable as our world turns. Through it all, thank You that I am Your child and I am not alone in this journey. In Jesus' name, Amen.

NOTES

DAY #29

What If...

◆ ◆ ◆

In life we have to make choices. Even if you don't make a choice that's a choice! Life came become daunting at times and often unpredictable. Like my eye injury. I often wonder what if I didn't go to Lake Lanier on vacation. What if I didn't get on that particular water slide. What if I didn't hold my nose while hydroplaning before crashing into the opposite side of the slide then my thumb would not damage my eye so severely. What if......is a rhetorical question we all ask ourselves after the fact of a tragic event. It's a normal reaction but we can't camp out and roast our marshmallows there.

See as Believers we really only have two choices amid seasons of trials:

1. Become more reliant on God and trust His process..or
2. Become more burdened and run away from God

This has been one of the most difficult seasons of my life. I've had viral meningitis, colon issues, severe flus, Bell's Palsy, Pneumonia, Vertigo, C.Diff, arthritis, back problems, and the list goes on and on. Now this eye injury. It reminds me of the apostle Paul's journey. As I look back, I can see how the Lord was preparing my faith for His good work. The burdens I carried made me stronger, made me more appreciative about health and life, and ultimately drew me even closer to the Lord. I am a living testimony of his goodness despite all these things the enemy sent to try to destroy me. It's much harder to see how God is using these things in the midst of our storms.

These trials could have tempted me to throw my hands up and walk away from my faith. My dad, who I just met 3 years ago for the first time, is not a Believer asked me during a visit this weekend: "Son...If this God is good..Why does He let bad things happen to good people like you?" This is a rhetorical question that has been asked since the beginning of time. My response is that I know God is ALWAYS good. We may not understand why He allows certain things to happen and it may not seem fair. BUT he can use the most tragic events and turn them around to unspeakable joy. One example is the crucification and resurrection of Jesus!

We live in a fallen world where good and evil exists. We will not be protected by everything even as a Believer. However we can face our adversity with a different mindset. A mindset of faith, peace, hope, and love despite the burdens we face. In fact I believe we are spiritual beings having an earthly experience. We are here to spread the love of Christ to everyone in every situation. Jesus said:

> *"I have told you all this so that you may have peace in me. Here on earth, you will have many trials and sorrows. But take heart, because I have overcome the world" (John 16:33).*

Notice Jesus said you won't have peace in your job, career, your children, marriage, friends, parents, pastor, car, home, or bank account....no...why? Because these things are subject to change at the blink of an eye or a poke of the eye in my situation...lol. That perfect peace is only found by putting all your hope in Jesus and the Father's love for you. He's the only one to live, die, and raised to new life to tell about it for 40 days before He ascended back to his heavenly home which is our home too!

What if.....you trust Jesus and What if....you find peace in Him in your current and all future situations! What an amazing promise! See we will not find lasting peace, forever happiness, or even a perfect life every second here on earth. The trials of life will come to us all whether spiritually, emotionally, physically, or financially. But we can find JOY in all those things and more through faith in Jesus Christ, who promises that he will never leave us nor forsake us. I'm not talking about religion. I'm talking about an intimate personal relationship with the one who designed us and everything good in this universe. He will be our protector and place of refuge when difficult seasons come. He will watch over his children so that nothing separates us from Him.

So when the What ifs...come in your life because they will... plant this scripture in your heart:

> *"For I know the plans I have for you,"* declares the Lord, *"plans to prosper you and not to harm you, plans to give you hope and a future" (Jeremiah 29:11).*

On Friday I'm moving forward with surgery on my eye. I'm believing that God will be directing and holding the surgeon's hand. It will be a quick surgery with no surprises. My eye will be restored back into health better than it was before. I'm believing with you that whatever situation you are faced with this season you will make the first and best choice, to turn to the Lord so that he can bring you out better than before.

My Prayer...

Daddy God, You are so gracious and kind to us even when we don't deserve it. Help us to remember all the deep pits you've pulled us out of. You are simply amazing. You love for us is eternal and everlasting. We are so fearfully and wonderfully made in the eyes of our enemies. Let our trials draw us even closer to You, so we can experience your glory on the other side of this mount. In Jesus name. Amen.

NOTES

DAY #30

*Walking Through The
Haze Of Change*

◆ ◆ ◆

As I prepare for my eye surgery tomorrow the doctor told me don't be surprised if I have a haze over my vision for a few days while waiting for change. Sometimes in life you will experience the same: a haze before change while waiting. This kind of change usually will not be a fast event. No. Oftentimes you have to simply walk through the process of it. God is more interested in the process of change verses the destination created by the change. Get that! See it's in the process where you mature, grow, and where your spiritual muscles are developed.

Some folks love change. They are thrill seekers....like my wife! Others dislike change. It stresses them out...like me....lol. Many even panic when the mere idea of change float across their minds. I get it, as a normal person, we all find change a little scary. It's human nature to want to know what's around the corner or behind the door. That's what makes the best horror flicks right? Lol. Then they end up being the one....well I won't go there in this inspirational message today!

Throughout life, we've experienced certain changes that feel better than others. You've finally delivered that baby after waiting 9 months. You've finally graduated from college or your child from kindergarten. You've finally opened your own business. A new career opportunity has opened up with more benefits and is less than 5 miles from your home! You say "Thank You God. I Knew You Were With Me!"

However what about the opposite: you got laid off from a job, a spouse walked out on you with no warning, an unfavorable medical diagnosis for you or a loved one or suffered an injury like my eye that prevents me from working and providing for my family. Now this type of change is stressful and leaves us baffled. We now question Where is God? Well He's with us through the haze of change good or bad. The Bible says God will never leave us nor forsake us. Jesus is the same yesterday, today, and forever (Hebrews 13:8). Emmanuel is another name for Jesus meaning God with us!

No matter the change we face, good or bad, stress usually travels with it. And as humans, we handle stress by looking for a way to cope with it. We try to find stress management books, systems, or listen to people giving us 10 steps of stress reduction techniques. Nothing is inherently wrong with this but the creator of the universe uses a different system of approach. He has given us 31 flavors like Baskin Robins on how to deal with anything in life on a daily basis. Where is it located? I thought you might ask. It's in his Word in the book of Proverbs. There are 31 chapters in the book of Proverbs. A chapter for each day of the month...with 3 extra if you need a little more in February. As an added bonus, every time you read it again you get something new!

For example Proverbs 16:9 tells us

"we can make our plans, but the Lord determines our

steps."

What an amazing promise. You mean Dr. Short in the middle of my haze of change the Lord will determine my steps? Yes. But He can't make them for you. That's where your faith kicks in. Not only does God determine your steps, He's walking with you as you make them. He's not looking out of his heavenly window spying on you to see if you will trip! The Lord knows every detail of what lies ahead in our life and desires for us to live life abundantly. Since that's true, then our task becomes less about knowing the outcome and more about knowing Him.

So we need to figure out what it means to walk with our Lord through the haze of change. We do this by staying close to Him and fellowshipping with Him. This looks like a morning of praise, prayer, worship, and surrender. It looks like scouring His word for the truth and understanding. Meditating on His Word throughout the day. Wandering in nature and observing the beauty of life. Being silent. Being alone. Sitting with the best counselor called the Holy Spirit. Opening ourselves up to another's wisdom. Inviting others to witness our struggles - That's why I've been so transparent about my eye injury journey. It's not so you can feel sorry for me. It's so you can see how to walk through the haze of change successfully.

When we seek to keep in step with the Holy Spirit in the midst of change, we're choosing to trust in our Lord and Savior. That's all God wants us to do. In Isaiah 43:19 God gives us an amazing promise while we are walking through the haze of change: "See, I am doing a new thing! Now it springs up; do you not perceive it? I am making a way in the wilderness and streams in the wasteland." Now that's something to do a few cartwheels over! Wooohooo! God got this beloved! He knows what's best for us and the proper timing to release it.

My Prayer...

Father, I don't know exactly how all this turns out. But I know it's going to be great! You've told me not to be afraid 365 times in your Word. You've redeemed me and called me by name. When I'm in rough waters, you will not let me go down. Teach me to simply be in Your presence while walking through this haze of change. Open the eyes of my heart to what You would have me to see in this season. Guide the surgeon's hand as he works on my eye tomorrow. I understand that sight is a precious gift from you. Give me the courage to continue to trust in Your goodness and grace. In Jesus' Name, Amen.

NOTES

DAY #31

Trusting Him 100%

◆ ◆ ◆

As a follower of Christ, things can be beautiful and scary at the same time. Many people know about Jesus. However, there is a big difference between knowing about Jesus and consistently walking in his ways. In order to follow Christ properly, we are called to trust Him in every situation we find ourselves in, good or bad. I know this is easier said than done. The cool thing is that you never have to do it alone. Jesus sent the Holy Spirit to dwell in us as Believers. He is our counselor, guide, comforter, and lets us know what's on God's heart.

Maybe you are dealing with a broken relationship with a family member, coworker, spouse or friend. Perhaps facing challenges you have no control over, like losing custody over your child, losing someone you know and love, facing a financial difficulty, struggling with self-esteem, or a sickness or injury has affected you like my eye accident. You may be adapting to a new season of life and find it's more difficult than anticipated. Trials and circumstances like these can cloud our focus and distract us from the Lord and what the Holy Spirit is calling us to.

Trials aren't inherently bad. They come to make us stronger

and bring us closer to God. That is the beauty of the gospel and that's why we need Jesus. Jesus said He Is The Door and Light. Nobody can come to the Father without me (John 10:9). This is significant because everyone is welcome. There are no prequalifications. No sins you gotta clean up. No church you must join. He loves you right where you are but cares too much about you to leave you there! He wants to be part of our everyday lives! When we trust the Lord, His love and grace is put on display as we become more like Jesus.

So what does trusting God look like? Trusting God is active listening to the Holy Spirit in our hearts and applying God's Word on a daily basis. It's usually a still quit voice that's not moody nor in a rush. I call it the unforced rhythm of Grace. Will you mess up? Absolutely! I still do and have been in it for 45 years. I'm sure I sin or miss the mark daily. However, I know I have perpetual forgiveness because of my faith in Jesus finished work on the cross. And so do you! That's an amazing gift! So as you navigate through the labyrinth of life, trust that God's ways are better than ours (Isaiah 55:8-9). Allow the Holy Spirit's work to transform us into the image of Jesus. That's the whole reason why God sent his only begotten son to dwell among us and ultimately live in us. Always remember the Christian life is less about feelings but more about relationships.

When we trust Jesus and cast our cares on Him, it leads to the miracles of God and displays His faithfulness. That's what I've been doing since day one of my eye injury. I've seen the hand of God move favorably on my behalf. Today is my first day of recovery from eye surgery. Is it uncomfortable? Yes! But I know it's just a short season and my best life is around the corner. Likewise whatever you are dealing with today: a new job, loss of a job, a new relationship, the loss of a relationship, gotten a good health report, gotten a bad health report, a promotion, loss of a promotion, etc...God is with you! In these times we must put our faith in action. The act of faith is our way of showing God that we fully trust Him and that we are giving Him full control of our circumstances and life.

My Prayer...

Lord, I thank You for bringing me safely out of eye surgery and on the road to recovery. You have given me the opportunity to encourage those who are floundering in their faith even during my trying time. Some may not know about the Good News of Jesus or the gospel. I thank You for the love and grace You have shown me to teach them so far. I thank You that you will continue to extend the same to those reading the messages of mine daily. Thank you Jesus! Because of you, we get to have an unbroken relationship with the Father because of your courage and finished work on that cross. Now God looks at us the same way He looks at you. Now Father give us the strength to trust in your divine plans and say "yes" to You, even when it is difficult so that You may be glorified in our lives. Amen.

NOTES

DAY #32

Prince of Peace

◆ ◆ ◆

Life has challenges that sometimes leaves you in the dark with blurred lines. Like my eye accident. Even though I went through surgery 2 days ago, I still have some blurred vision and considerable pain. Is it time for me to worry? Or Is it possible to find peace even still in the midst of uncertainty? What about your situation? Today hear Jesus speaking these words over you:

> *"Peace I leave with you, my peace I give to you; not as the world gives do I give to you. Let not your hearts be troubled, Neither let it be afraid." -John 14:27*

The world will not ever give you this type of peace. It doesn't have it to give. It's like getting blood from a turnip. So be careful because the world system will allow money to give you a false sense of peace and security. However it can't solve deep problems in the heart and minds of people. Drugs can't do it either..no matter if it's legal or not.

This is the type of peace Jesus offers:

- *The peace that defies circumstances.*

- *The peace that defies logic.*

I can remember thinking how in the world is that even possible? I get it. For someone who has never experienced it sounds cray. I'm a living witness of it now. It's been almost 2 months I've been out of work due to my eye injury. With no income yet bills are still coming in. It feels like my ship is sinking and sinking fast. I don't have an associate in my practice and still paying my staff to be there. They have families and expenses. I promised them I will keep them on payroll as long as I can. Hopefully until I get back to practice if that's God's will for me. However God has provided and has brought people to walk this journey out with us. We are very thankful.

However, we are not at the end and my situation still requires incredible trust and peace. Jesus is the only one that can give me the peace that defies circumstances and logic. That's why Jesus is called the Prince of Peace! He can speak one word and calm the winds and waves in your life, he's also an anchor for our souls— and He can do the same thing with your heart that's full of fear, doubt, unbelief, anxiety, and depression.

So how do you get this peace and remain in it? It's when we are focused on Jesus and remain in his rest, our minds will be fixed on His peace. Peace is found in trusting the person who controls all the things.

Colossians 1:16-17 says:

> *"For in Jesus all things were created, things in heaven and*

on earth, visible and invisible, whether thrones or dominions or rulers or authorities. All things were created through Him and for Him. He is before all things and in him all things are held together." What a powerful promise!

Today Meditate On:
His Great LOVE.
His Eternal GLORY.
His Infinite WISDOM.
His Unwavering FAITHFULNESS.
His Perfect RIGHTEOUSNESS.

Jesus is the Prince of Peace prophesied in Isaiah 9:6 and will always remain in perfect peace (Hebrews 4:14). He's seated at the right hand of the father making intercession for us (Mark 16:9). We are spiritually seated in Jesus as well right now (Ephesians 2:6). What amazing promises we have in Christ Jesus!

So I challenge you, find peace in Jesus today. This is what's been keeping me sane the past 32 days since my eye injury. God has allowed people to come along side of us with support. It's been amazing! So once again, keep your eyes on Him and off your current situation you can't control. Jesus will provide a type of a peace and a way out that people will be confused by. That's the kind of crazy peace and reckless love YOU are called to in Him.

DR RICO D SHORT

NOTES

DAY #33

Keep Doubt Out

I'm finally on the road to recovery and it isn't easy. My two eyes now have to talk to each other as well as my brain. Yes the surgery is done but the pain is still present. That's how life works as well. The pain sometimes may make you think something went wrong but pain can often be the precursor to healing. I'm 3 days post-surgery on my eye and yet it feels like the day I injured it. However, I know that's a natural part of the process.

The enemy whispers see Dr. Short you aren't healed. If you were, you would not still be in pain. Or he'll say your eye will go back to the awkward position soon. Or your run of 20 years in dentistry is over and you will lose everything. Or your gonna have a lazy eye..etc. Do you know what I do when the enemy starts talking trash? I quote bible scriptures to KEEP DOUBT OUT. For example, I say by Jesus stripes I am healed, as Jesus is so am I in this world, my God shall supply all my needs according to his riches and glory in Christ Jesus, beloved I wish that you prosper above all things even as your soul prosper, I am the head and not the tail, I'm a lender not a borrower, Jesus will perfect the things that concern me, God owns the cattle on a thousand hills and all the gold and silver is mine says the Lord, God who gave us Jesus freely will not withhold any good thing from us...should I keep going? This is the treasure the Bible talks about in earthen vessels. We are the earthen vessels and the word of God is the treasure!

This is how to keep doubt out. Recite the Word of God over your situation. The Word of God is sharper than a two-edged sword and able to cut apart soul and spirit. It goes down to the marrow where the red blood cells are produced that gives us life. It produces the precious gift of peace amidst the storms of life. Check out Apostle Peter and the other disciples when they were in a storm. Jesus walked on water passed them as they were panicking. Peter was the only one with enough courage to step out of the boat right during the middle of a treacherous storm. He sights were set on Jesus and began walking toward Jesus on top of the water. He defied the law of gravity and buoyancy. This shouldn't really be that much of a surprise.

Jesus created the laws of nature. Everything is held together even down to the atom by Him. As long as he focused on Jesus, he was at peace and oblivious to the stormy waves that were crashing around him. This is how I'm able to stay sane after 48 days with no income, can't practice, and not sure of my future in dentistry. I know as long as I keep my eyes on Jesus, I can defy laws of nature as well. It's when you allow doubt to come in that's when sinking takes place.

As soon as Peter took his eyes off of Jesus and focused on what was going on around him, he became fearful and he ended up getting swallowed up by the waves. This is a life principle! What are you afraid of? That contract not going through, that health situation your mom or dad is facing may not turn around, finances getting low, got laid off and it's holiday time, afraid of the holidays because that's when you miss your loved ones who has passed away the most, etc.

Beloved our feelings or circumstances may not change right away, I get it, but our attitude can. Find His perfect peace in the midst of uncertainty and doubt. Just like Peter had to lose his fear and take a giant leap of faith to step out of that boat we must be willing to do the same if we desire to walk in the fullness of what God has in store for us. See Jesus ain't gonna snatch us out of the boat and make us walk on water. Nope. That's not his nature. However, he will call us to trust him and take the next step on to the troubled waters. See as Believers, God never called us to stay in our comfort zone. That's low living. God calls us to go higher in Christ! The high life. We are called to go beyond our comfort zone to reach the peace and comfort that only Christ offers. Jesus even said we will do greater things than he did! Don't believe me? Go to John 14:12

> *"I tell you the truth, anyone who believes in me will do the same works I have done, and even greater works, because I am going to be with the Father."*

You may be thinking now Dr. Short you've taken this too far...nope! It's what the Word says. We haven't seen it manifested because we don't really believe it. Listen! Honestly, the world is waiting for us to put on the Jesus peace... (in my Kanye voice). The world cannot give us Christ's peace, and it can't take it away from us either.

Right now, in this moment surrender your doubts and take up peace in Christ. Just simply close your eyes, lift up your hands, shift your focus from your problems and put them in Jesus hands. Your deepest fears and anxieties become no match for the power and faith found in Jesus. You will rise up and stand on the waves of chaos and move toward your divine destiny on earth. The only person who can stop you is you. The choice is yours.

I encourage you to find the confidence and boldness in God's presence today. Take that step out in courage. Let go of all the fearful things trying to hold you back. You are a lion from the tribe of Judah. You are fearfully and wonderfully made. The world is waiting on you to move into your position of power, influence, and authority with the Holy Spirit leading and guiding you. Don't worry about the waves of people chattering about you and hating on you. God's power is in you and all around you. That's all you need. So receive the peace that Jesus is offering you today. Keep doubt out. Jesus will calm the waves. Trust Him. He's rooting for you.

NOTES

DAY #34

Let The Lord Fight For You

◆ ◆ ◆

In life nothing is guaranteed. We will all face challenges. There will be battles you will have to fight and ironically some you don't. But how do you know the difference between the two? It's by spending time in prayer and in God's Word. As a Believer, we are automatically armed with spiritual weapons to pull down any strongholds we face and diffuse the devil's lies (2 Corinthians 10:3). The Holy Spirit living inside of us arms us with a sword, the Word of God, to stand tall when the enemy attacks us mentally, physically, relationally, emotionally, or financially. Jesus equips us with strength, wisdom, and discernment through The Holy Spirit to stay strong in the spiritual warfare battle.

During this eye injury journey I have been under attack in many areas and it hasn't been easy. In fact, I'm still dealing with issues as I heal from the eye surgery. Things like will I get to practice again, will I be able to provide for my family at the same level, will I lose what I worked so hard for over 15 years, will I be able to make up for over 2 months of loss income, what happens if my fine motor skills are altered from the injury, will my referrals start back sending me patients, does God want me to do something different, will I have to sell my practice, or will I have to start over from scratch?

These are just a few questions relating to the battle that takes place in my mind on a daily basis. Then I ask myself, what can I do at this present moment while these questions are bombarding my mind with fear and trepidation while waiting to heal from this eye injury? Then I stumbled across an old promise in the Bible. A precious promise and treasure for all those who are of faith facing a battle in life. It's found in Exodus 14:14 and it says:

> *"The Lord will fight for you, and you shall hold your peace."*

Peace is a gift from God. Totally free. No clearance tag. No religious hoops to jump through. His peace is only achieved when you are wholeheartedly seeking Him.

This is so powerful! The creator, sustainer, and most powerful being in the universe is on our side. See it's really simple. We make it complex. When we hold on to our peace, God fights for us. Read that again! This peace isn't a feeling or emotion. It's a real live person. His name is Jesus. He's our anchor during the storms of life. How do we hold on to someone we can't see? I knew you would ask. We hold on by trusting Him, holding on to his promises to us, and keeping our eyes on his finished work. We simply ask Him to enter our "ring" just like a wrestler would tag his partner when he gets in trouble. Then we just wait and watch Jesus work WWE style!...lol

If you're a believer who is living like salt and light in the earth, your faith will be tested. Trust me I've been through it and got many battle scars to prove it. You won't go for long without encountering spiritual warfare - obstacles and attacks that will be hurled at your direction by the enemy.

Jesus even said it will happen. God warns us to stay aware of Satan's schemes, to live alert in this crazy yet beautiful world, and to stay close to Him. As we do that we stay armed and ready. He invites us to spend time in His presence, through prayer and worship, pressing in to know Him more. As we grow to know God's truth and what is real, we also know more what is false. This gives us an advantage over people in this world who do not have a personal relationship with Jesus. We are stronger to stand against the attack of the enemy in the powerful name of Jesus. He never leaves us like an orphan to fend for ourselves in a dark world. No way! He reminds us He is constantly with us, fighting for us, even when we cannot see it.

So you may be asking how do I activate these spiritual weapons given to me? One way is to pray God's words back to Him. This is a powerful weapon against the forces of evil. It is Truth going out into the atmosphere. For example say: God you said you will perfect everything that concern me, God you said by Jesus stripes I'm healed, God you said I am more than a conqueror through Christ Jesus who strengthens me, God you said I will lend and not borrow, God you said you will keep me in perfect peace as I keep my mind on thee. When you make it personal - You Said- it reminds God of His covenant between him and Jesus on your behalf. Get that! It builds our faith and our trust in God. It guards our hearts and focuses our minds back on Him and off the battle. It wins the battle because our Lord fights it for us!

Today, remember, if you didn't start this battle...It's not yours to fight. The battle belongs to the Lord. Your job is to remain at peace or labor to enter in the rest of God. This is found in the finished work of Jesus. See the world can't give you this kind of peace, and the world can't take it away. (John 14:27)

I'm praying for you, that these truths flood your heart and continue to flood mine as I continue to walk out this eye injury journey by faith. No matter what you are facing...a sickness, financial instability, emotional stress, marital issues, stress on the job, stress in your home or at your church....my friend, you are loved more than you could ever know and God has the solution way before you had the problem.

So I challenge you today, look for peace from God in His Word. Talk to Him. Remind Him of His promises. Invite Him in the situation. Jesus died so we can have an absolutely abundant and amazing life here on earth even in the midst of our trials.

NOTES

DAY #35

A Miracle In Transition

◆ ◆ ◆

In life we will experience transition. It's unavoidable. We love transition from being single to being married. From college to a career. From an injury to health. From death to life. From being broke to having paper....lol.

To "transition" is the process or a period of changing from one state or condition to another. The Latin term for transition is "Transire" meaning to go across. Other definitions of transition can be described as a Movement, a Passage, or a Change from One Position to Another or a Paradigm shift. These are great when it's toward the positive but what happens when it's the other way? Transitioning from being married now divorced and single, losing your career you spent years learning in college and graduate school, going from health to an eye injury like mine in a blink of an eye, or going from more than enough income to no income in 2 months like I'm dealing with currently. What are we to do when the tides turn to the negative? When you lose a loved one? Now going from life to death. Unfortunately, many times life doesn't give us warning sings when these happen. And we aren't fully equipped to handle these situations when they occur.

Jesus can create totally relate to all these issues. He felt all of our pains and disappointments including all the highs and lows in life. He sympathize with us and our daily journey through life. However he can directly relate to us. How? It's because he is the definition of transition, he's called the way, the truth, and the life (John 14:6)! He's also called the door (John 10:7). The door is symbolic of transition..a movement, a passage, or a change where miracles take place. Not only is Jesus transitional but he's transformational!

Do you feel alone or abandoned? Beloved, some of the things or people that have left your life was for your good! Just because you are going through a difficult season doesn't mean God forgot about you. He said He will never ever leave us. The gift that God has given you is still present inside of you but may be lying dormant just for a moment in time. Just like a bear in hibernation. The power is there but it's resting and recharging for something greater! That's what I believe is happening during this eye injury journey of mine. See when you are in transition it's difficult to see it. When you transition from one season to another you plug into the same power but maybe have to use a different outlet. It's the same power who is God but a different source... a new position, a new career, or a new location. Did you know your curling iron uses a different outlet than your refrigerator?

It's designed that way for safety and proper power for the best result. Likewise with God. God said he will never leave you nor forsake you but he can change forms. Remember God is not a man but a spirit. He is still your source but may change your resource. Your job isn't your source, nor your parents, nor your spouse. These are all resources. God is our true source. In fact, God isn't always concerned about our comfort. Nope. He loves us too much to leave us in the same place doing the same thing for 30 years. He's more concerned about developing is more into the image of Christ. This will be challenging and will require transitional moments. See the way He provides for you in one season may not necessarily be the same way he provides for you in the next season. This isn't to hurt you. No. It's to mature you. It's to grow you up. You can't stay baby Christian forever. You have to get off the milk onto the meat. You can't be a professional athlete with a milk-based diet and perform at the optimum level. It won't work.

Furthermore, the relationships he gives you to support you in one season may not be the same for the next season. He may cut some of your friends off like hangnails...to the quick quick!..lol. Just because they leave doesn't mean God has. Beloved, the most important thing you can do during a transitional season is redirect your focus. Get that! Redirect Your Focus! Take your eyes off of what was to what is to come! Put those eyes on Jesus and experience the miracle in transition! Many of the miracles that happened in the Bible happened in transition moments.

* Did you know when Jesus fed the 5,000 with 2 fish and 5 loaves of bread, he was in transition. He was trying to escape the crowd yet they were waiting for him on the other side and they were hungry (John 6:1-11).

* Did you know Jesus was transitioning while on his way to heal Jairus daughter when a woman with the issue of blood reached out to Him as He was walking by. She touched the hem of his garment then the bleeding immediately stopped and so did Jesus. He said who touched me when there were hundreds touching him at the same time. He said no...somebody touched me with an unusual extravagant kind of faith! I felt power discharge from me! He applauded her for her courage (Luke 8:40-48).

These are just a few of the greatest miracles in the Bible and they happened in transition moments. I can go on and talk about the paraplegic that interrupted Jesus's sermon when his friends lowered him from the roof. Jesus not only healed him but forgave him of his sins as well even before he went to the cross! Some others are:

* Jesus Raising Lazarus from the dead

* Joshua and Caleb bringing the children of Israel into the Promised land

* God feeding the children of Israel with manna and quail in the Wilderness

Some of the greatest miracles in your life will occur during a transition period.

It's not when you get to your destination. Nope..right smack dab in the middle. When you least expect it....BAM! GOD likes to cut you off right in the crossroads of your normal journey. It's not to hurt you. It's to bless you. He doesn't want you to use your own plan. If you do you have to use your own power! But if you wait for his plan you'll receive his power to execute his plan. This means being still oftentimes and waiting.

I believe you will experience a transitional miracle during this time of uncertainty in your career, finances, marriage, or business. God isn't gonna do it when you think. It's gonna happen out of nowhere.

The difficulty in life we experience is learning how to shift gears when things get unfamiliar. Oftentimes we remain stuck because life isn't automatic. Nobody teaches you how to shift when transition moments happens. It's learned from experience. You've heard experience is the best teacher right? It's true and leads into the best testimony.

Oftentimes the gift shop is set up at the exit of an amusement park. Just like at Disney World. When you leave their Mickey knows how to get your money....especially while exiting. This place is where the enemy sets up shop to steal your joy, to steal your peace, to steal your stability. It's near the exit. It's also the transitional moment where the gift shop or treasure shop is located. If you have been under attack lately like me during this eye injury, it might mean you may be coming out of a transitional moment with plenty in 2020! With many gifts and treasures in your hands. Loaded down with very nice parting gift so you can remember who gave you the victory during the trial...Jesus!

Can God be setting up a blessing for you in this transition season? I believe so! Some of you are transitioning professionally, relationally, and spiritually into something beyond your wildest dreams. The way you manage your transition moments determines the magnitude of the miracle you will experience.

NOTES

DAY #36

Mind Games

◆ ◆ ◆

It's Day #36 since my eye injury and the battle for my peace hasn't let up. Every day the enemy comes with some sort of new mind game trying to create stress. He's saying: "What's going to happen to your practice Dr. Short?...What's going to happen to your beautiful home you believed God for? ...I thought you said God was going to make a way for you...it's been two months...he ain't showed up yet...I thought you said God was going to supply all your needs according his riches and glory in Christ?...He ain't doing it now! You haven't worked nor had over two months, you know your expenses are sky high, and your savings is being drained. You can't handle this anymore...just give up and quit Rico!....See you ain't the root canal specialist to the stars....you ain't no root canal specialist period anymore!"

I'm reminded Satan aka the enemy played the same mind games with Jesus while he fasted 40 days and 40 nights in the wilderness. Jesus was at his lowest point. He was hungry, frustrated, and tired. He put himself in our shoes in Matthew 4 so I'm in great company. Satan said to Jesus:

> "If you are the Son of God, tell these stones to become bread."

> "If you are the Son of God, throw yourself down. For it is written: " 'He will command his angels concerning you, and they will lift you up in their hands, so that you will not strike your foot against a stone.' "

> "If you will bow down and worship me, I will give you all the kingdoms of the world and their splendor."

Thankfully Jesus passed the test by not only quoting the word of God to the enemy in its context, He was The Word of God in flesh!

Sooner or later you will encounter a war with the enemy especially as a believer. It may be in your health, finances, marriage, relationships, on your job, in your home, at your school, or even at your church. He will play mind games. What will you do? How will you fight? Will you use God's words or the world's words? It's your choice.

Allow me to help you learn how Jesus fought back in Matthew 4 and take notes:

> "Jesus answered, "It is written: 'Man shall not live on bread alone, but on every word that comes from the mouth of God.' "

> Jesus said to him, "Away from me, Satan! For it is written:

'Worship the Lord your God, and serve him only.' "Matthew 4:4, 10 NIV

He trusted the Word of God over everything else. Ironically he was The Word of God but still trusted in the written word of God! In addition, He told Satan to jet! At times our minds will be prone to recklessly roam all over the place especially under stress. Where our mind is, our words and emotions will follow. What have you been thinking about lately? Are you complaining or are you praying? Are you in fear or are you in faith?

I'm in day #36 of this eye injury journey and I'm learning peace isn't the absence of problems. Peace comes when you stop looking at the problem and start looking at your Heavenly Father. Colossians 3:2 says

> *"Set your minds on things above, not on earthly things".*

See I've learned as we focus on the problems we are facing; the peace of Christ becomes out of focus. The perfect peace offered through Christ has no room to exist. Focusing on the problem clouds your mind which clouds your emotions and now causes stress which causes you to make bad decisions. The Bible says to take all those negative and worrisome thoughts captive and make it obedient to Christ (2 Corinthians 10:5). That simply means put Christ in your situation and see how he would respond. The Bible also says we have the mind of Christ (1 Corinthians 2:16). Satan or Stress no longer has to have any influence over us if we are operating within the peace offered by Christ.

Are you stressed now? With everything going on around you especially during the holiday season take time and memorize this verse:

"Be still and know that I am God." - Psalm 46:10.

That's it. Simple.
Don't allow the enemy to hijack your mind and life. Just Focus on God. He's the author and finisher of your faith. He knows you by name. You are the apple of his eye and the focus of his affection even on your worst day!

No matter what you are going through right now God's plan will always override the enemy's plot. Don't fret. Don't be dismayed. God is fighting for you as you read the words on this page. His battles are often won in silence. One day you will wake up and just like that it's over! You've come out more blessed, healthier, more prosperous, more influential, and with a mind of peace. The Prince of Peace, Jesus, has won once again! He is inside of us to stay no matter what comes our way! What an amazing promise we have!

So I challenge you today, Take those worrisome thoughts captive (2 Corinthians 10:5), pray for guidance, and trust that God will provide peace in your world full of chaos. Nothing is too hard for God. No sickness, no disease, no eye injury, no financial difficulty, no marriage issue...all these things must bow at the name of Jesus! So don't shuffle along with your eyes to the ground, absorbed with the negativity right in front of you.

Look up and be alert to what is going on around Christ—that's where the action is. See things from his perspective. You are in Him and He is in you. I believe and declare your situation will change!

NOTES

DAY #37

Waves Of Doubt

If you are a human being you will experience waves of doubt. One thing, after another, after another. You are being bombarded by the issues of life. I call it a "Tsunami Of Life Trials". I experienced that as well 2 days after my eye injury in September.

My daughter Ava who is 12 years old almost died. We ordered takeout at one of our favorite Chinese fast food chain restaurants. While sitting at the table she complained her throat was itching after the ate her normal sting bean chicken with rice dish. Later on that night she was racked with abdominal pain. Immediately I thought it was appendicitis but she started blowing her nose profusely. Her eyes started watering and then she could hardly breath. We gave her Benadryl and Ibuprofen just because that's all we had. My wife used her mother's intuition and said let's take her to the emergency room. While in the car her throat started to close and she was going into anaphylactic shock. Fortunately, there was no one on the Emergency Room on the child side at 1am at Kennestone Hospital. They immediately took her back and gave her several doses of epinephrine. In addition to Albuterol. It was not working. They were ready to airlift her to Children's Hospital of Atlanta because her situation was declining rapidly. I was praying for her. Yes in panic mode…I ain't gonna lie….lol.

IN THE EYE OF A STORM

A parent's worst nightmare is unfolding. Fortunately by the grace of God they were able to stabilize her. The next day, she visited her allergist. We discovered there was cross contamination by accident with a peanut dish at the CHINESE restaurant. Ava is severely allergic to peanuts. Between my eye injury and Ava's brush with death from a peanut allergy that was more than enough waves of doubt to sink a ship! A Tsunami Of Life Trials!

During this tumultuous time, I still had to find a way to stay encouraged. I had to keep looking up from feeling down. Maybe you are going through waves of doubt now. Don't give way to the waves of discouragement or doubt. Our Heavenly Father has graciously chosen us to give us everything we need at the proper time even at when we feel as if our ship is sinking like the Titanic.

This message is for you. You who are facing waves of doubt in your marriage, family, health, or finances. You who is longing to see God do "a new thing" in your life or business. Oftentimes We wonder why me God? When will you change my situation?
Or Why did you change my situation....I was comfortable!
Trusting God when waves of doubt are crashing in your mind one of the hardest lesson to learn, but it is also the most crucial.

You may think for a hot second trusting yourself can oftentimes be easier than trusting God. Ok..Mr. Big Shot go ahead. Can you see around corners? Can you walk through walls? Can you speak and calm waves of doubt and disbelief? Probably not as good as Jesus.

Beloved, remember that God loves you too much to answer your prayers halfway. There is a perfect timing to all his answers. We just have to trust that He knows best and have our very best interest at heart.

He knows your needs, wants, and your desires — He put them in your heart! So allow Him to use His to us His perfect wisdom, His perfect timing, and His perfect knowledge to bring them out. In order to develop his best portrait of you must require time in the "dark room". If you are under 35 like the 35mm film....don't worry about it...you're too young to understand how camera film was developed pre-smartphone. God is the only one that can truly fulfill His plan for your life. It's bulletproof. He longs to give you a peace that will never die nor fade away.

Flowers die.
Dreams die.
Marriages die.

But faith in Jesus and his finished work never ever dies. It's always full of life! Everything lives in Christ. He's The Resurrection! He's The Way, The Truth, and The Life. Jesus gives us a perfect peace that changes everything...including us.

> *So stop trying to define peace and comfort by your own standard. It's too small and fleeting. On the contrary, start defining it according to God's standard. It's Big and long lasting. Jesus said in Matthew 6:31-33 "So do not worry, saying, 'What shall we eat?' or 'What shall we drink?' or 'What shall we wear?' For the pagans run after all these things, and your heavenly Father knows that you need them. But seek first his kingdom and his righteousness, and all these things will be given to you as well."*

My prayer today is that you trust Him, even in your waves of doubt or in your Tsunami of Life Trials. God has your best interest in mind and desires to manifest himself in your darkest moments. The stars only shine brightest among a dark backdrop. Continue to rely on Him for guidance and peace. Remember that

God created the concept of time and can live in time and outside of time at the same time. Meditate on Jeremiah 29:11 today "For I know the plans I have for you," declares the Lord, "plans to prosper you and not to harm you, plans to give you hope and a future."

<u>NOTES</u>

DAY #38

The Panic Button

Most people don't stay calm while sinking in quicksand. We scream and yell! We hit the panic button. Unfortunately there are some people who still hit the panic button while they are on concrete. They worry all the time. They "think" they are in quicksand. Believers in Christ shouldn't have a panic button. They should have a praise button! Child of God, you must remember God stays true to his Word during life's toughest moments.

We may wonder...Where is God? Why hasn't He helped me yet! See God knows your life from the beginning to the end and everything belongs to Him. "The earth is the Lord's, and everything in it, the world, and all who live in it;"(Psalms 24:1). He knows where you will be successful and know where you will struggle. He wired you purposely to depend on Him always in all ways. That's why we should talk to him or some call it Pray to him. Praying isn't begging God to do something for you. Praying is developing a personal relationship with your Heavenly Father who knows all of your sins but still loves you like Jesus. Yep! Did you know that?

IN THE EYE OF A STORM

<u>God loves to hear from us. He loves to answer our prayers with grace and wisdom.</u>

Season's change, but His love and peace remains towards us the same simply because of Jesus finished work on the cross.

It's Day #38 for me and my eye injury journey. By the grace of God, the pain has eased but the nausea and boat sickness really hasn't. I was at the Atlanta Falcons game today and I don't know what made me feel worse...my nausea sense surgery or the way the Falcons played today against Tampa Bay! Lol.....
Anyway, I'm trusting that He's working in the background for me and hopefully my Falcons. I know He's repairing and lining up the nerves, blood vessels, and eye muscles in perfect working condition. You may not be going through an eye injury but perhaps you are going through something...What season of life are you walking through?

Because at the end of the day, we are all walking, jogging, running, or crawling through something today.

Life can be full of...
Good times.
Bad times.
Times filled with sorrow.
Times filled with laughter.
Times of success.
Times of failure.
Times when things are easy.
And times when things are just downright hard.
It's just the ebbs and flow of life.
(Ecclesiastes 3:1)

However, I'm so thankful we have a promise that won't disappoint us. A peace that frees us from difficult times and goes beyond understanding! Jesus is that promise. So don't be surprised if things get worse before they get better. It's part of the divine plan. At some point, God will deliver you out with more than you had before. God is the king of glory and is fighting for you. "Who is this King of glory? The Lord strong and mighty, the Lord mighty in battle"(Psalms 24:8). We can confidently rejoice because things will get better.

While in the midst of the storm, we may cry, complain, blame, or be in the depths of despair, like I did for the first month of this eye injury but the beautiful thing about it is that Jesus is always near — and He proves His peace that surpasses understanding every single time!

In our worst moments we can still have hope, peace, and joy because we have someone fighting for us in the background. The pain you are experiencing now is only temporary. God's love and peace for you is permanent. If you are in a tough season like me, remember the old saying: "this too shall pass". Weeping may endure through the night but joy and peace comes in the morning. (Psalm 30:5) So turn that panic button into a praise button because you know all things are working together for your good. Those who seek God and inquire of his goodness will make it without any doubt. He's at their side GOD. it.

So I challenge you today to find joy knowing that Jesus died and rose again so that you and I could live an abundant life of peace, love, and kindness on this earth no matter what we are facing today!

NOTES

DAY #39

Count It All Joy?

◆ ◆ ◆

Have you ever been in a trial for a long time? Maybe like me almost 2 months with an eye injury? Or more and you can't see light at the end of the tunnel? The doctors say give it more time. Your friends say you just need rest Doc or God knows how to sit you down because you've been too busy lately. I know this sounds cliché but it can work your last nerve!...especially when you don't have income coming in. If I was sitting on a few mills or a few tickets that would be a lot different (a mill and a ticket is slang for a million dollars) By design I don't have a lazy bone in my body. I want to go work and provide for my family and continue to be a blessing to others. And enjoy the lifestyle I worked so hard to attain by the grace of God.

Such prolonged trails have a unique way of emotionally and spiritually wearing us down. Negative thoughts swirl around in our heads. Anxiety creeps in. The enemy tries to take advantage of our vulnerability and pain. He throws lies and accusations in the mix. Like "You should have never went on vacation with your family, "It was their fault you got on that water slide causing your eye injury", "You should not have told the young girl behind you in line at the water slide that it's going to be fun and no need to be afraid", etc. It's the same when he tempted Adam and Eve and tried to tempt Jesus. He prowls around, waiting for just the right moment like a bloody, injured deer to devour us. Little does he know as Believers; we have blood on us alright. However not the blood of a deer, it's the blood of Jesus! No weapon formed against us shall prosper (Isaiah 54:17). We are more than conquerors in Christ who gives us strength (Romans 8:37).

No matter how hard it gets, we must not lean into our own understanding or listen to our own confused thoughts or the devil's crafty lies (Proverbs 3:5). This will lead us off course and take our eyes off of the Lord. Our attention becomes divided and we become distracted. We end up sinking like Peter did when he took his eyes off Jesus. The Bible talks about a double minded man won't see the promises of the Lord because they are unstable (James 1:7). Doubt sets in followed by discouragement, depression, and even despair. We can't let that happen to us! Every day as we awaken we must find something to be thankful for! God is working in the background to bring us to the foreground!

James 1:2 tells us to count our trials all joy. I know...if you are thinking like me...WHAT? This hurts. I don't like it. It's taking too long. Get me out of this season pronto God! Some translations actually say count it "great joy" and another says "pure joy"! Pure joy? How in the world can we count our prolonged periods of suffering as pure joy? James is looking deeper than our narrow understanding of our trials. He was the brother of Jesus. He saw him personally in public and in private. He saw how he dealt with difficulty that the bible didn't record. It was always with grace and trust. He understood that trials bring something unique and spiritual into our lives that nothing else in life can.

Trials test and refine the gifts the Holy Spirit has given to us.

Trials produce patience in our lives in dealing with others.

Trials are used by God to produce a greater anointing in us.

Trials attract our angels to work supernaturally for us.

Trials allow God's glory or kavod to rest on us.

Trials will result in a great reward for us in heaven.

All of these benefits are certainly reasons to rejoice and count it all Joy! Philippians 4:4-8 says:

> *"Rejoice in the Lord always. I will say it again: Rejoice!"*

It says it twice! So that tells us something happens very powerfully when we rejoice in the Lord. I believe it becomes like spiritual dynamite. It changes and rearranges things for our good. Does your current situation need some power or rearranging? Does something needs to be changed In your marriage? In your finances? In your home? In your career? Dealing with that co-worker? Dealing with that mother-in-law that's always in your business and never wants to go home...lol? Put on some praise and worship music and just have a Jesus party! "And the peace of God, which transcends all understanding, will guard your hearts and your minds in Christ Jesus" (Philippians 4:7). He will revive and refresh as you while changing your situation as you spend time in His Word (Psalms 119:28).

"Consider it nothing but joy, my brothers and sisters, whenever you fall into various trials. Be assured that the testing of your faith [through experience] produces endurance [leading to spiritual maturity, and inner peace]. And let endurance have its perfect result and do a thorough work, so that you may be perfect and completely developed [in your faith], lacking in nothing." (James 1:2-4 AMP)

NOTES

DAY #40

*Rejoice in the Lord—
Always....In All Ways?*

◆ ◆ ◆

Whatever you are going through this is a key to your breakthrough. REJOICE IN THE LORD! It's something I've done daily before and since this eye injury. I know you are thinking even in times of affliction, distress, or persecution? How can I celebrate? It's because we know that God has a plan in our afflictions. Don't forget that! Everything He allows to enter our lives He has a divine purpose and working together for our good. That's why we can indeed rejoice right in the middle of it!

Beloved, God is Good. Don't let your current situation make you think that He isn't. He is full of compassion, merciful, and kind. All He allows in our lives comes from a heart that is wise, wonderful, and worthy of praise. Trust me, I know it's difficult to see it when you are in the throes of life like me on this eye injury journey but God promises to deliver us according to His Word in Psalm 119:170. We usually want *out*, but so often it is the Lord's love that wants us *in*. Often times the trial has been designed by Him out of His deep love for us....to fashion us to be more like Jesus....to perfect us for His glory....not lacking any good thing..to take us higher than we've ever been before! You remember Job? He got double for his trouble! That's why we can REJOICE!

Child of God, let me encourage you He will never leave us in the storm alone. So in the midst of the deepest, longest, toughest trial, you can know that He's in it with us. A ship has never sunk with Jesus on board and no one ever died in his presence. He created the water the ship floats on and the law of buoyancy! He is the Resurrection and Life. The Bible says we will never plumb the breadth, the length, the height, or depth of His love for us. And when our strength is at its weakest point and we can barely lift our head, our tender Shepherd will light the way. He will allow someone or something to encourage us and tell us we are moving in the right direction. Don't turn back now! That's why we can REJOICE!

We can also rejoice because of what Jesus has done for us. He has secured a mansion in heaven with our name on it for eternity. There will be a heavenly party everyday with no sickness, lack, or jealousy! Because Christ is the same yesterday, today, and forever; His grace is always sufficient! His love never ends and He has delivered us from the kingdom of darkness into the kingdom of light! Jesus blood has washed away our sins - past, present, and future! He is the light at the end of the longest, deepest, and darkest tunnel of our trials. That's why we can REJOICE!

So each morning when you wake up, even if you don't feel like it or your situation hasn't changed much..like mine...I'm just being transparent....Rejoice in the Lord anyway!

Tell him Thank You because He is good all the time and is working all the time for our good and His glory. Make it a point to rejoice in this way you and I promise you will be surprised at the results! The joy you have in God will provide renewed strength and grace for the day. It will energize and galvanize you! It will light you up like a Christmas tree! It will give you a reason to keep going in the midst of your trial. Apostle Paul said,

> *"Rejoice always, pray continually, give thanks in all circumstances; for this is God's will for you in Christ Jesus." (1 Thessalonians 5:16-18).*

The joy of the Lord is indeed our strength. That's why we can REJOICE!

NOTES

DAY #41

Entrust Your Trial To The Judge

◆ ◆ ◆

Isaiah 33:22 says The LORD is our Judge, the LORD is our Lawgiver, the LORD is our King; it is He who will save us. Your trial is divinely set up by the King of Kings who will always rule in your favor. His name is Jesus! So in the middle of your trial Give it All to Him with Thanksgiving! Are you facing a trial now? Instead of being anxious in our trials of life, we are to take all of our needs and requests before the Lord. He's a just judge and desires to know all the details of your case. Tell Him: the who, what, when, where and why.

I know what you are thinking....well Dr. Short since He's God doesn't He know everything? Yes. He knows everything. But, He wants to hear it from you. This creates relationship and intimacy which is what He's after. He has seen everything you have gone through and has never left your side. In fact, He knows you even better than you know yourself. He put you together. He knitted you in your mother's womb (Psalm 139:13). You're not the invention of your parents. You just came through them! When we truly bring these things to the Lord, lay them at His feet and walk away, the peace of God will keep our hearts and minds. What a mighty promise!

So what are you afraid of? You have nothing to lose and everything to gain. Give everything that concerns you over to Him. Your current health situation, marital problems, financial crisis, and lack of purpose. Place it all into His sovereign hands. The all-powerful, all-wise, and loving care of God created you and He cares for you. You may have to this more than once and that's ok. He never gets tired of hearing from you. Some days it might seem as though you are having to entrust your cares to Him over and over. That is okay. That is exactly what He wants us to do. In our weakness He is strong. He loves working with us through our darkest moments. And guess what else is good? Our sins don't disqualify us from receiving his goodness. Jesus dealt with our sins once and for all on the cross when He said FINISHED! In fact the Bible says where sin abounds, God's Grace super abounds! (Romans 5:20)

The Bible says ironically that we are to bring our requests to the Lord with thanksgiving! I know this sounds confusing. How am I to be thankful about going through this trial? Right...I get it. See God's kingdom is set up as an upside-down Kingdom. Many times it's the opposite of what we have been taught in life and how the world operates. The Bible refers to idiosyncrasies like the greatest person is a servant to all, the last will be first, count it all joy when you fall into trials, etc. When we offer thanksgiving to God in the midst of our trials it creates gratitude in our hearts. This gratitude spills over and change the way we look at the situation. All of a sudden the problem seems smaller than it really is. This is because we stop amplifying the problem and magnifying the solution. God is good. God is wise. God is kind. God is love. He is all of these things all of the time to us and for us through Christ. Get this...Anything He permits is filtered through His goodness, wisdom, kindness, and love. He's more concerned in developing you in the process than getting you to the destination. Trust Him. He knows best—always. It may not be an eye injury you're dealing with like me but it could be an issue with your confidence, self-esteem, appearance, or personality. The trials you are facing isn't to hold you back. No my friend. It's to change you and thrust you forward with the help of an all-powerful judge on your side. So Rejoice! And give thanks!

NOTES

DAY #42

Think On The Truth

❖ ❖ ❖

Believe God' Word and Trust His Promises. When going through a tough situation in life this is crucial. It sounds simple. But it is not easy as it sounds. Many times throughout the day our mind races with thoughts of the past failures and future stress. Very seldom we are quietly composed in the "now". See, the current moment is the only thing you can somewhat control. At least in thought that is. This is the place where the Lord wants us to be more present. That's why it's called the present. It's a gift, to be cherished and not taken for granted.

Oftentimes when life throws us for a loop we are confronted with a choice. Whether it's an eye injury I'm currently healing from, a financial set back, a marriage on the brink of divorce, a business close to bankruptcy, a recent layoff, a career change, or even losing a loved one you have the option to choose where you will place your hope. It is the choice of whether or not we will humbly trust the Lord and believe His Word or live in frustration and despair. It is the choice of whether or not we will believe that God is good, that His promises are yes and amen, and that He will always keep them regardless of our current situation...even if it's our own fault. It is the choice of whether or not we will receive these promises by faith—

He is my God.
He has my best interest in mind.
He wants me to live my best life.
He is good to me always.

This has to be affirmed over and over and over in your mind daily. It's already in your spirit because God put it there. But the two must work synonymously in order to be effective. However, there will be times that you will doubt that these promises are true because the situation will scream louder than these truths. Human nature kicks in and fear tries to kick out faith.

Questions, decisions, and choices will arise throughout the day as we experience the tough trials. Don't be surprised when finding yourself challenged, tested, and tempted around the questions of who God is, His love for you, and whether or not you can fully trust Him in the midst of the current difficulty. You and I are not alone. Jesus disciples dealt with the same situation. Jesus fed multitudes of thousands with a few fish and chips two times yet his disciples still didn't trust him 100 percent. So don't beat yourself up if you feel insecure. You will have multiple moments in life to put his love and trust for you to the test.

What we think matters and is directly connected to His promises. Proverbs 23:7 says

> *"As a person thinks in his heart, so is he".*

How we think about God and His Word changes us from the inside out. In the midst of great trial, logic and faith can leave us fast like a hummingbird bird flying away from our window. When this situation happened to my eye, I thought my career was over. After the surgery, I still have a ways to go in order to see properly. However, I can now see light at the end of the tunnel. I believe I will be able to practice again. It's been over two months since dealing with this eye injury and out of work but feels like two decades.

When we suffer with a loss for a prolonged period it can be so hard to hold on to the truth of God's word. So we must be very intentional daily on reading and studying it. We must make it a point to stand firm and think on truth not our feelings. Our feelings lie like a rug and change like the seasons. We must believe what the Bible says about who God is and rest in Jesus finished work.

Change will happen my friend. Either the situation will change, we will change, or a combination of both. Jesus said his yoke is easy and his burden is light. He bore all of our sins, situations, and diseases on the cross. It's by his stripes we are healed. God has also given us the mind of Christ to be free from guilt, condemnation, and anxiety. We must cling to what the Scripture says about us rather than believing our feelings. Also don't trust the conclusions by drawing from other people's situations. They aren't our exact circumstances. We don't know exactly what they were thinking and how they were applying God's word to their situation. It's not our business either. This is critical to understand. The enemy will have you more focused on what didn't work out for someone else in the same situation as you are in verses the truth of God's word! Don't fall for this old trick.

Beloved no matter what situation you are facing today, believe God's promises for you. Embrace them in hope as if it's a life preserver in the middle of the sea. If hope is all you have left, you are holding on all that's right. Rest in the promises of God and don't rush his process of developing you in the situation. When we do this our situation will change and we will be stronger than ever before. Keep your eyes fixed on Jesus and your minds on his promises because they are "Yes and Amen!"...in Christ (2 Corinthians 1:20).

DR RICO D SHORT

NOTES

DAY #43

The Waiting Period

◆ ◆ ◆

Have you ever been tired of waiting? Waiting for a loved one to be healed of cancer. Waiting to get back to work after an injury. Waiting to get a call back from a job interview. Waiting to receive the results from your test. Waiting for that loan to be approved. Waiting for your child to figure life out. Or like me waiting to see the Ophthalmologist for the progress of my eye after surgery in order to get back to work.

Waiting isn't very comfortable. It can be mentally and emotionally draining. However, I found a powerful truth in the Word of God regarding waiting. Romans 8:22 says "Waiting does not diminish us, any more than waiting diminishes a pregnant mother. We are enlarged in the waiting. We, of course, don't see what is enlarging us. But the longer we wait, the larger we become, and the more joyful our expectancy." This is such an awesome promise for those of us who are waiting for a breakthrough in our situation! The longer the wait the larger the blessing.

For example, the gestation period for a dog is 63 days and they give a litter on average of 6 puppies. On the contrary an elephant is pregnant for 608 days and give only one or two max baby elephants at a time. So if it's taking longer than usual, get ready because you are getting ready to birth something BIG and uncommon!

Today I want to give you 5 practical steps during your waiting period.

STEP ONE: START EVERY DAY TO REJOICE IN THE LORD!

Find something to celebrate with God about. It can be something as simple as being clothed in your right mind, got food in your fridge, and clothes on your back. Know that God has a plan in our trials and purpose in every situation we face. He permits some things to happen in our lives to grow us and mature us in his Word. This is how we become strong and look more like Jesus. Because of this, we can indeed rejoice! We can also rejoice because of what He has already done for us in Christ. We are more than conquerors in Christ (Romans 8:37)! Because we have Christ, no matter what negativity is going on around us, it doesn't have to get in us.

STEP TWO: ENTRUST YOUR TRIAL TO THE LORD.

Many times we want to be our own judge and jury. We want to fight issues in life on our own. Let me tell you this kind of fight will wear your out. It's like shadow boxing yourself and expecting your shadow to get tired. Instead invite God into your ring. Share all the details of the match to the Lord and confess your desired outcome to him. Hebrews 4:16 says "Let us therefore come boldly to the throne of grace, that we may obtain mercy and find grace to help in time of need". The word boldly means without reservation, apprehension, with full confidence. Once you have shared all of the details of your trial with the Lord, entrust Him with them. Don't pick them back up again trying to fix it. And each time that issue pops back up in your head, make it to be thankful for something God has already done for you. This confuses the enemy and refuels you're tank of faith. He got this. Trust Him. He knows best—always.

STEP THREE: THINK ON TRUTH DURING THE WAIT

While waiting it's normal to get tired. Then doubt will try to creep in your mind. Saying things like "If God was going to fix it, he would have done it by now!" This is another trick of the enemy. Romans 8:26 says "Meanwhile, the moment we get tired in the waiting, God's Spirit is right alongside helping us along." The Holy Spirit is an ever-present help. He's God's spirit that Jesus sent as he ascended back into heaven. The Holy Spirit is our counselor and guide. He helps us during the wait. You may say I don't even know what to pray Dr. Short. It doesn't matter because he will help us in that too. In fact, just a groan can reach the throne! Romans 8:27-29 goes on to say: "If we don't know how or what to pray, it doesn't matter. The Holy Spirit does our praying in and for us, making prayer out of our wordless sighs, our aching groans. He knows us far better than we know ourselves, knows our pregnant condition, and keeps us present before God. That's why we can be so sure that every detail in our lives of love for God is worked into something good." What a blessed assurance!

STEP FOUR: GUARD YOUR HEART

I know you may be thinking how do you guard your heart. Do you remember that first date? You opened your heart wide open after that first kiss to that guy then found out later he was a jerk! Since then you've been guarding your heart. Well it's similar when it comes down to the enemy tactics. We must choose not to listen or engage in any thought that does not line up with the Word of God. That's how we guard our heart. Proverbs 4:23 says: "Above all else, guard your heart, for everything you do flows from it." Our mind is connected to our heart and we must protect it because it's prone to wander to dark places. We must keep it on course by meditating on the Word of God daily during our waiting period.

STEP FIVE: RELAX AND REST

This sounds like a good idea but how do I do this in a trial and I'm waiting. Well sometimes you gotta talk to yourself. No this won't make you seem crazy unless you do it in front of people of course. Check out what the psalmist wrote in Psalm 116:7-8 "I said to myself, Relax and Rest. GOD has showered you with blessings. Soul, you've been rescued from death; Eye, you've been rescued from tears; And you, Foot, were kept from stumbling."

He literally spoke a commanded blessing over himself. He spoke to his soul when it was in despair, he spoke to his eye when his vision wasn't clear, and he spoke to his foot when he was lost needing direction! Beloved, it's not your job to figure everything out despite what your parents may have told you when you turned 18. No! Rather than trying to figure everything out, just fix your eyes on Jesus. See whatever God has promised gets stamped with the YES of Jesus (2 Corinthians 1:20). God affirms us of all his promises by making us a sure thing in Christ.

The Holy Spirit is our official stamp of His YES within us. Because of this we can be assured whatever he started in us He is destined to complete through us. Humbly, obediently, and faithfully follow Jesus. Not your pastor. Not Kanye West. Not Justin Bieber. Follow Jesus. He's the author and finisher of your faith! Joshua 21:25 says

> *"Not one of the good promises which the LORD had spoken to the house of Israel failed; ALL had come to pass."*

As a Believer, we are the spiritual house of Israel. The true and loving God resides in us because of Jesus finished work on the cross!

NOTES

DAY #44

Created Fearless

◆ ◆ ◆

"I praise you because I am fearfully and wonderfully made; your works are wonderful, I know that full well" Psalm 139:14. God is with us. God is for us. We'll be Victorious. God made us Fearless.

Just on that you can give a great shout to the Lord! God is love and God is power. All day long God's promises of love pour over you and me. We may not see it or feel it but it's true. Through the night and during the day He is singing songs of praise over us. If you don't know any songs to sing back to him it's ok to create your own. I believe he personally enjoys that even more! This is a powerful type of prayer to God. So if you are feeling depressed or in despair speak to your soul in singing prayer.

> *Psalms 42:11 says "So I say to my soul, "Don't be discouraged. Don't be disturbed. For I know my God will break through for me. Then I'll have plenty of reasons to praise him all over again. Yes, living before his face is my saving grace!"*

The Bible describes God so full of love for us – His created beings – that it's too much for us to even comprehend. It's so wide, so high, so deep we won't even be able to comprehend it in eternity. He showed us this love by sending his only son Jesus to die for the sins of the whole world - past, present, and future.

This isn't a religion. This is a relationship. In this perfect love for us there is no room for fear. This is critical for you to understand. His word says that "perfect love drives out fear" (1 John 4:18). So when fear grips your heart tightly we know there is a disconnect in understanding the love that God has for us. As I'm writing this I'm guilty of being fearful at times as well...especially during this eye injury journey. I love Romans 5:8. It's the evidence of God's love for us.."But God demonstrates his own love for us in this: While we were still sinners, Christ died for us."

It's vital for us to understand God knows about all of our fears. He came down as a man in the body of Jesus. Jesus felt stress and fear as well so we are in great company. Luke 22:42 bears this out. Jesus prayed "Father, if you are willing, please take this cup of suffering away from me." You talking about stress! The Bible also records Jesus was so stressed he sweat blood in Luke 22:44 "He prayed more fervently, and he was in such agony of spirit that his sweat fell to the ground like great drops of blood." This was before his crucifixion. Hematidrosis is a real medical condition that causes you to ooze or sweat blood from your skin when you're not cut or injured under immense levels of stress. The capillaries in the skin burst and combines with sweat that oozes out the pores. Only a few handfuls of hematidrosis cases were confirmed in medical studies in the 20th century.

God himself knows our fears as He felt them in the body of Christ. He promises us His "peace that surpasses all understanding and guards our hearts and minds in Christ Jesus" (Philippians 4:7). So imagine fear like a toothless Rottweiler. All bark but no bite. Once you put your trust in Jesus, fear like this toothless Rottweiler, can only "gum you alive"...lol. Because of Jesus finished work on the cross we don't have to live under the yoke of fear any longer! He will never leave our side and in his presence there is fullness of joy which cripples fear. His unconditional love is always making all things new for you!

So spend time in God's Word and allow his promises to cascade over you today. Constantly seek His presence. This is how we stand strong during times of fear. We all will face fear and challenging times in this life. But we have the ability to walk in confidence and fearlessly take more territory for His kingdom. God has not given us a spirit of fear but of power, love, and a sound mind (2 Timothy 1:7). Beloved we have the amazing gift and responsibility of bringing light into the dark corners of this earth. Fear has no chance against those who's confidence is in the Lord.

NOTES

DAY #45

The Number 45

◆ ◆ ◆

I was raised as an only child from a single parent household. Life was hard growing up but it made me who I am today. I've faced many tests and trials in my 45 years on this planet but nothing like the one I've shared with you in this book.

When I was conceived my mother said I would be a special child. Why? Simply because I gave her heart burn and made her nauseous while she carried me for 9 months....lol. On top of that, she said I was a very difficult delivery. She would not ever get back on the birthing table again. Well she is still a woman of her word. I am still her only child.

Before I was born and conceived, I knew the Lord had a special plan for my life. Out of all the millions of sperm that could have fertilized that one egg, I made it to the finish line first. The Lord chose me and appointed me my name. My mom had no real reason to name me Rico on 6/29/1974 my birthdate. It wasn't after anyone famous, no one was Hispanic, nor my father whom I didn't know at the time was named Rico, or anyone she had known. In fact, I wasn't supposed to be here. I was conceived out of wedlock and planned to be aborted. However, God designed it otherwise and said nahhh...not this one. Since I've been a young adult, God gave me a gift of communication. In His kindness, God has allowed my gracious words to penetrate the hearts and minds of all people. He inspired me to write a book in 2011 called "Getting To The Root Of Your Problem: 365 Days Of Inspirational Thinking". The book has done extremely well over the years and has allowed me to speak in many placed over the world. As a self-published author, who had no idea what I was doing, the book has sold many copies worldwide.

I've always wanted to write a few more books but never had the opportunity until now. God has kept his hand of protection on me for 45 years and I'm forever Thankful. He said to me, "You may not know your earthly father. But you know your heavenly one, You are my son. I will show my glory through you. I will also make you a light for other nations. Then you will make it possible for the whole world to see the beauty of Jesus in your work by healing and teaching others the grace life all over the world. The joy of the world's salvation, named Emmanuel or Christ will be in you." Ironically the name Rico means glory in German. In Spanish it means wealthy, delicious, abundant, full, and lovely. The **number 45** is a blend of the energies of 4 and 5. **Number 4** signifies instinct, inner-knowledge, wisdom, creating foundations, helping others, hard work, ability, being stable and dependable, and success. **Number 5** signifies God's grace and unmerited favor found in Jesus finished work. It also has energies of redemption. Eyes haven't seen nor ears haven't heard all the things God has planned for me and you since you have read this 45-day journey of inspiration. My prayer is for you to be encouraged and enlightened as God continues to provide peace in the eye of your storm.

NOTES

ABOUT THE AUTHOR

❖ ❖ ❖

Dr. Rico D. Short is a board-certified endodontist, author, and speaker. In addition, he is an expert spokesperson on Endodontics for the American Dental Association (ADA), a professional organization representing approximately 161,000 U.S. dentists.

Dr. Short has over 20 years of experience in dentistry and over 15 years in endodontics. He is a member of the Fellow International College of Dentist, a graduate of the ADA Institute of Diversity In Leadership Program, and an ADA Success Speaker. He is also an expert consultant in endodontics to the Georgia Board of Dentistry and an assistant clinical professor at The Dental College of Georgia in Augusta. Dr. Short is an independent national lecturer and is endorsed by the American Association of Endodontists speaker's bureau. Furthermore, he is an opinion leader on various dental products before and after they hit the market.

Dr. Short has written numerous articles and published in several journals including Dentistry Today (He made the exclusive cover April 2013), Inside Dentistry, UpScale Magazine, Rolling Out Magazine, and the Journal of Endodontics. In addition, he has published over 1,000 articles on social media involving case studies in endodontics. They are called "The SHORT Case Of The Day" in which he has a robust worldwide following of over 100,000 dentists.

Dr. Short has lectured at the American Dental Association several times and the National Dental Association annual meetings. He has lectured at local and large state meetings including the California Dental Association and others throughout the United States and the Caribbean. Dr. Short's work has been published in dental journals around the world with opportunities to speak in China and the Philippines. Dr. Short was named one of the Top 40 Dentist under 40 in America by Incisal Edge Magazine in 2013, Top 20 Alumni Under 40 by Augusta University, and has been named in Dentistry Today consistently as one of the top leaders in continuing education.

Dr. Rico Short attended the Medical College of Georgia School of Dentistry (The Dental College of Georgia) to attain a Doctor of Dental Medicine Degree in 1999. In 2002 he earned his post doctorate degree in Endodontics from Nova Southeastern University. Dr. Short added the final notch to his belt and became a Diplomate of the American Board of Endodontics in 2009. His private practice, Apex Endodontics P.C, was opened in 2004 and is located in Smyrna Georgia just outside Atlanta.

Dr. Short has received several prestigious awards and accolades throughout his career. He is very philanthropic in his community. Dr. Short has established an annual scholarship at The Dental College of Georgia in Augusta, formally known as The Medical College of Georgia School of Dentistry. He is an American Dental Association Success Speaker and a graduate of the Institute of Diversity and Leadership Program. With this knowledge, Dr. Short travels around the country speaking to senior dental students about the future of dentistry. In addition, he volunteers at various non-profit organizations and charity dental clinics. In October 2012, Dr. Short was selected as a panelist for the Affordable Care Act. He was invited to The White House to give his personal opinion about how The Affordable Care Act would affect both businesses and citizens of our country from a healthcare provider perspective.

Dr. Short is also a motivational speaker and author. His new book entitled "Getting to the Root of Your Problem" 365 Days of Inspirational Thinking is considered one of the most thought-provoking self-published books to date. He travels abroad teaching people to tap into their God given potential to make a positive difference in society. Dr. Short is married to Angela Short who is a dental hygienist. They have two children Jayla and Ava.

Made in the USA
Columbia, SC
22 December 2019